The Untold Realities *behind the* Unseen World

Kelliote S. Kadammanja

ISBN 979-8-89243-415-7 (paperback)
ISBN 979-8-89243-416-4 (digital)

Christian Faith Publishing
832 Park Avenue
Meadville, PA 16335
www.christianfaithpublishing.com

Printed in the United States of America

DEDICATION

I feel privileged and humbled to dedicate this book to the church of the Lord Jesus Christ, the very community that He has established and continues to raise up even to this day. The church is the body of Christ and through it, God accomplishes His divine purposes on Earth.

I am grateful to be part of this community of believers, and I pray that this book will be a valuable resource to the church as we strive to grow in our understanding of God and His ways. May the church continue to be a shining light in a dark world, bringing hope and salvation to all who are lost and in need of a savior.

CONTENTS

FOREWORD

God has a unique purpose and mandate for every individual, which is to live a life of worship and to always recognize His presence among us. However, many of us fail to acknowledge His presence in our daily lives. I believe that God employs various means to draw our attention to His presence, and this manifests in different ways for different people. His desire is for us to attain our ultimate goal of eternity, as stated in John 10:28.

This book contains numerous revelations that the author has been blessed to experience through vivid encounters with God. It is not common for individuals who encounter such vivid expressions of God to freely share their experiences unless God Himself allows it at His own time and in His own ways. I believe this detailed account of God's interaction with Kelliote would greatly benefit readers in understanding the various ways in which God reveals Himself and protects and communicates with His beloved children, as stated in 1 John 3:1.

Enjoy the various encounters and manifestations of God's love and protection to mankind.

Evangelist Dr. Kholiwe Mkandawire
Vet surgeon, pharmacist, lecturer at Lilongwe University of Agriculture and natural Resources, Malawi

ACKNOWLEDGMENTS

I am deeply grateful to the grace of God for giving me the privilege to be among those He uses to impact others through this book. It is not something I take lightly, but rather with a heart full of gratitude.

Moreover, I want to express my sincere appreciation to those who supported me throughout the journey of writing this book. Your input, ideas, and resources were invaluable, and I couldn't have done it without you. Erik Grehl, Esther Chikuse, Dr. Kholiwe Mkandawire, Justin Kantchentche, my family, Joseph Zulu, and Charlotte Kalua, you have my utmost gratitude for your contributions. Your support has made a significant impact on this book and will undoubtedly touch many lives.

INTRODUCTION

The life of a believer is highly valued in the eyes of God, yet many of us are unaware of this truth. God desires that we attain a level of understanding where we comprehend His ways and purposes for our lives. As stated in Hosea 4:6, "My people are destroyed for lack of knowledge." This implies that if we had knowledge of what God has in store for us, we could remain steadfast, safe, and secure.

By the grace of God, I have been fortunate to receive spiritual insights and learning that few others have been blessed with. I have shared my personal life experiences with various individuals, communities, and congregations, and I have received both positive and negative feedback. Despite the different reactions, I have learned to give thanks to God for every opportunity He has given me to bear witness to His goodness.

Throughout the years, I have received a lot of heartening feedback from individuals who have read and heard my testimonies about God and the spirit world. I truly believe that the realities you will find within the pages of this book have the potential to bring about significant transformation in your life as well. It is no coincidence that you have chosen to invest your time in reading this book. I am confident that God had you in mind when He allowed me to witness His power and goodness, and I am excited to see the impact it will have on your life.

I had been yearning to share my experiences with others by writing about them for years. However, the Holy Spirit urged me to be patient and wait for the appropriate moment. Those who are familiar with me may question why I've kept it hidden for so long. I am delighted that the appropriate time has come, and I believe that it will have a significant impact for the glory of God.

In the pages of this book, I aim to share some of the experiences I've had in my life, alongside those of my friends who also witnessed the supernatural events that we experienced together. Through my own life journey, I will demonstrate how God has been with me in powerful ways, just as He is with every one of us. My hope is that this book will serve as a reminder to all of us that God is always present with us, even closer than we may have ever imagined. By sharing these personal encounters, I believe that we can all grow in our faith and deepen our understanding of God's presence in our lives.

As you read, keep in mind that nothing can be more important than God's Word, not even visions or dreams or any supernatural experience. My own experience has taught me that it's crucial to value God's Word above all else, even over spiritual encounters, visions, or other manifestations.

The reason for this is that without understanding God's Word, these experiences can lead to confusion and even be harmful instead of being helpful. As you read, you'll see that I've included biblical references to some of the experiences. You may even be able to relate to them with your own scriptural references.

I want you to know that I'm no different from any other believer, and these experiences could happen to anyone that God chooses. Sometimes people expect too much from me after reading or hearing my testimony, but it's not about me—it's about God and how He chooses to work through each of us. The truth is that whatever happened, it didn't happen just for me. It happened for anyone that God chooses to show His greatness and purpose for humanity, all for His own glory.

CHAPTER 1

The Background

I was born and raised in Malawi, a small country located in southeastern Africa. Malawi has three main regions, and I spent most of my childhood in the southern part of the country. Later on, during my teenage and adult years, I lived in the central part of the country.

When I was growing up, my parents made sure that I attended church every Sunday and tried their best to teach me about God's Word.

However, as a child, I didn't really understand the importance of it, especially since I grew up in a rough neighborhood surrounded by tough kids who influenced me to behave like them. This was my typical life until I turned twelve years old when God began to build a personal relationship with me.

When I was in eighth grade in 2009, I became born again, which means that I believed in Jesus and accepted Him as my Lord and savior.

Despite my decision to follow God, I still had doubts about my faith at times and wondered if I was truly born again. Then something interesting happened after I did well in my eighth grade national exam. I was able to attend the school that I had always wanted to go to because it was one of the top secondary schools (high schools) in the entire country and it was a boarding school.

During my first term at the school in 2010, an evangelist visited and held a preaching session one Wednesday night. Before the preaching, he showed us a movie called *2012*, which was a 2009 production depicting the apocalypse, supposedly taking place in the year 2012.

The evangelist said that his intention in showing us the movie was to provide an idea of what the end of the world might look like since the movie had depictions from the book of Revelations in the Bible. As I watched the movie, it scared me immensely, prompting me to reflect deeply on my life.

Regardless of whether the world was actually ending in 2012 or not, the movie made me contemplate the fact that the end of the world would eventually come and determine the fate of my afterlife, whether I was alive or not. This realization prompted me to consider making an unwavering decision to follow God for the rest of my life, which could ensure my safety and well-being. Making that choice didn't hurt at all. After the movie, the evangelist preached and invited those who wanted to believe and follow God to come forward, and I was among those who went to the front.

From that time on, I had a desire to know and experience God more in my life than ever before. I developed a passion for the kingdom of God and to learn more about Jesus. By the end of year 2012, I had studied almost the entire Bible with great curiosity to understand the ways of God.

I read numerous accounts about various Bible figures ranging from Noah, Abraham, and Moses to many others throughout the Bible. It is truly astounding how what may appear to be mere Jewish literature can captivate your comprehension in a unique manner and revolutionize your life in a powerful way more than any other stories you may have read. By delving into these narratives, I began to understand God and His capabilities more intimately. I sensed that I genuinely had faith in that same God and that He still wields the same power as He did in ancient times.

Getting to Know God

Despite learning about the ways of God during those years, I still perceived Him as distant from me. I believed that being young and inexperienced with matters concerning God hindered me from developing a close relationship with Him. I thought that I hadn't achieved much in life to impress God, and that He only drew near to those who had accomplished great things, like the Bible figures. In my mind, I imagined that God had a ranking system for all Christians based on their strength, years of being born again, level of service to Him, or other criteria that I had not met.

I believed that I had not yet earned the right to have a close and intimate relationship with God. Although I knew that God was great and powerful, I never expected to experience His manifestations up close. I thought that the experiences of those who had a strong faith in God in the past were not meant for me, as I felt inadequate. According to my mind, I needed to accumulate more spiritual experience before I could have a meaningful relationship with God, and I believed that this could only happen when I was much older. I assumed that I would only experience God's power when I had reached a certain level of maturity.

I discovered later in life that as a Christian, I did not understand the following scripture: "But now in Christ Jesus you who once were far away have been brought near through the blood of Christ" (Ephesians 2:13 NIV).

Before, I hadn't comprehended the grace of God that I received through the blood of Jesus. As a Christian, I was already in a close relationship with God since Jesus's blood is near to Him. It wasn't until around 2012, when I was fifteen years old, that God started to work on me to understand His ways and how much He loved me, just as He loves everyone. That's when everything began to change for me.

If you are experiencing the same sentiments as I once did, you have come across the right information at this moment. Within the pages of this book, I can attest that much of the knowledge regarding the spiritual realm was acquired directly from God. I have not had the privilege of being mentored or instructed on a personal level, apart from learning from others at a distance.

I have come to realize over time that many of these lessons are intertwined with the teachings found in the Bible. As you delve into this book, always keep in mind that no vision or dream is greater than the Word of God. The Word of God is the ultimate authoritative resource at our disposal.

Getting to Experience God

God started revealing things to me through my dreams, where I would see events that would happen later on. Some people might think this is normal, as they may have also dreamt about future events, but for me as a teenager, it was amazing how accurate my dreams were. My dreams would show things about my personal life, my family's future plans, as well as general news that would happen in the world.

In some of my dreams, I saw presidential elections that I had no prior knowledge of. I didn't even know that these countries had elections coming up. However, God showed me the results before they even happened. At that time, I didn't follow politics because I was a teenager and had no interest in it. I thought watching the news was something only old people did, so I didn't pay attention to it.

The first dream was about the United States presidential election in 2012, which was going to happen that year. In my dream, I saw Barack Obama winning the election, and I was watching it on a news channel called France24. The news said that Barack Obama won the presidency for the second time.

I was surprised because I had no prior thoughts or information about it. Curious, I decided to search for information on my small Nokia keypad phone with a broken screen that could at least connect to 2G internet and opened Google. I found out that there were indeed elections coming later that year. As the year went on, the election happened, and it turned out exactly as I saw it in my dream. I realized that God was sending me a message through my dream.

I had a similar experience with the Zimbabwe presidential elections. I wasn't following any current affairs of Zimbabwe, so I wasn't expecting there to be elections. However, my dream accurately predicted that Robert Mugabe would win, which surprised me because of the negative perspective people had of him in the country, yet it happened exactly as I saw it.

These are just a few examples of how God revealed His ways to me. As I continued on my spiritual journey, I learned to cultivate a habit of prayer and to connect with God personally in my private space. The more I spent time in fellowship with God through prayer, the more I began to receive insights about future events that would come to pass in the world. These revelations would come to me while I was awake and praying, rather than in my dreams.

You might wonder how I knew that the things flashing through my mind during prayer were revelations from God. The answer is simple: John 10:27–28. Jesus spoke about how His sheep would recognize His voice, and that is exactly what happened to me.

If you are connected to God, you will be able to recognize when a revelation comes to you, whether it's through a voice, pictures in your mind, or even just a feeling. This is because, as Jesus said in John 10:27–28, His sheep know His voice.

Whenever I received a revelation, I would share it with those around me, such as people I prayed with, so we could pray together about the vision.

In 2012, Malawi was facing economic challenges. The country had experienced a 3.5 percent growth rate in its economy in the previous years. However, the president at the time refused to allow some influence from western donors as he believed their requests were immoral for the country.

This caused the donors to cut their donations to the country. As a result, the country did not have enough foreign currency to have enough buying power in the international market for most of the important imports like car fuel. This, in turn, caused social unrest.

The president passed away due to cardiac arrest, which resulted in the vice president assuming the presidency. Under the new president's leadership, relationships were mended, and everything began to fall back into place. People were delighted as the new policies appeared to be highly effective, leading to a drastic shift from a poor situation to a good one. However, during my time spent in prayer, I had a vision that contradicted what everyone else was seeing on the ground regarding the future of the country.

In one of our prayer meetings, I shared with the people present about the upcoming economic situation in Malawi. Despite the government's efforts to improve the economy and the positive outlook of the public, I had a vision that the value of the local currency would decline significantly, and specific prices for some products would skyrocket. Some people were skeptical and found it hard to believe.

After I shared my vision, someone approached me to express their doubts because they believed the government's policies were effective. However, about two years later, Malawi faced its most severe economic crisis to date, leaving the country in a vulnerable state for years to come. Even as I wrote this book, the country was still experiencing the repercussions of the crisis.

At the time when I was having these revelations, I was in grade 11. I shared these things with people during various prayer meetings that took place at the school where I was studying. The school is called Likuni Boys' Secondary School, and it is located in the central region of Malawi.

As I experienced these revelations, I got more and more confirmation of the presence of God in my life. I knew that God was personally involved in everything I was experiencing. Knowing that He was speaking to me and revealing things to me caused me to draw even closer to Him. He continued to reveal Himself to me, even though I never deserved this or expected it. God reveals Himself to us in many ways sending different signals such as dreams in my case.

In my view, these are messages from God, as He communicates with us in unexpected ways. I urge you to ponder over the messages that you have been receiving from God in your daily life and discern their significance. Initially, I was perplexed as to why God would reveal to a young local Malawian teenage boy, matters concerning American politics that seemed irrelevant. I later realized that it was because God knew that you, the reader of this book, would derive a lesson from it and grow closer to Him. Let us now proceed and discover what occurred subsequently.

CHAPTER 2

The Beginning of God's Manifestation of Wonders

During my holiday breaks from school, I enjoyed watching television and was particularly moved by individuals who acted as vessels for God to demonstrate His power in the lives of others. As a high school student, I would often yearn for the opportunity to return home and catch up on all the TV programs I had missed.

We had a satellite receiver, and I had memorized all the frequency numbers for free-to-air channels which were mostly Christian. During holidays, I would spend most of my time watching these channels as they were a source of inspiration for me. Moreover, they were helpful in allowing me to sit and learn from other Christians from around the world.

Observing others serving God fueled my desire to learn more about His power and greatness, and how it can manifest through humanity. I longed to be filled with God's might, just like the ministers I saw and those who had strong faith in the Bible. Conversely, I believed that they were more uniquely special to God than I was and never thought that I could be like them someday.

As I learnt the Word of God more and more, I discovered that, as believers, we are all partakers of the grace that God has given as a gift to those who believe in Jesus Christ. I was just waiting for a chance to exercise what God had given me as a believer even though I had some doubts, which kept me out from exercising my faith.

Since the time I received Jesus Christ as my personal Lord and savior, I was committed to affiliating myself with groups that would help me grow in my Christian walk. One of the groups that I joined at the school was SCOM, which is an acronym for Student Christian Organization of Malawi.

SCOM is a Christian organization that was founded in 1961 in Malawi and focuses on helping students grow in their faith. It is primarily run by students in their respective schools, with oversight from leaders who are part of the parent organization. SCOM is present in most high schools, universities, and colleges in Malawi and has had a significant positive impact on the lives of many students, including me.

In my first year of joining SCOM, I was pleasantly surprised to receive an invitation to a leadership workshop for SCOM leaders organized by the parent organization, despite not holding a leadership position within the group. It was a great feeling to be acknowledged by the senior leadership as a potential future leader, especially since I had only attended SCOM prayer meetings and nothing much.

After some time had passed, I was selected to become one of the leaders when I advanced to the next grade level. This newfound role provided me with the chance to minister to my fellow students, although I was quite nervous initially. As time went on, I was able to master my public speaking skills and used them to serve God's purpose. This ultimately led me to the spotlight where I continued doing the work of God within my school.

The Trigger of God's Power

After observing my ability to share the Word of God at SCOM meetings, a friend approached me for help. We sat down together, and he confided in me about a problem he was facing, seeking guidance and support.

During our conversation, he informed me that he had been experiencing memory loss and painful headaches, which were causing him a lot of distress and negatively affecting his studies. Some may question why he came to me for help instead of seeking medical attention, given the severity of his symptoms. In our Malawian context, individuals from low-income backgrounds like myself and my friend would not immediately consider seeing a doctor as their first option, as such healthcare services were often perceived as being exclusively and easily accessible to the well to do. In most cases, head scans were only carried out in emergency situations.

As my friend shared his struggles with me and explained how they were impacting his life, I felt a deep sense of compassion for him. I offered words of encouragement and shared passages from the Bible to lift his spirits. I was so moved by his predicament that I felt compelled to do more to help him. Nevertheless, I had at no time prayed for anyone before, so it took a lot of courage for me to ask if I could pray for him for the very first time.

My friend agreed to let me pray for him, and we scheduled the prayer session for early the following weekend. We decided to meet on a Saturday morning since it was the only time we could find a private place to pray without interruption. With most students resting in their dormitories after a long week of school and mandatory lone studies, it was a quiet and secluded time for us to pray together. I felt relieved that we could escape from any potential persecution or scrutiny that might have arisen had we prayed during the week when others were around.

When Saturday morning finally arrived, I felt nervous about what was going to happen during the prayer session. To calm my nerves and build up my faith, I armed myself with many Scriptures. I spent time reading and confessing Bible verses that were relevant to the situation at hand.

We decided to leave the dormitories and meet in one of the classrooms. I encouraged my friend to have faith in Jesus and His power to heal.

With faith in God's ability to change my friend's situation, I prayed for him for a longer time, of course asking God to show up and transform his story.

After some time of praying, he suddenly began to respond to the prayer. He started shaking and crying as the power of God fell on him. As I continued to pray, I was amazed to see that it was through me that the Holy Spirit was touching him. I was so excited that God had shown up that I briefly smiled while praying for him as he shook uncontrollably and cried.

After the prayer, he felt liberated, and he later told me that he went behind some trees within the school premises and prayed alone with an uncontrollable sense of joy. From that moment, the problems of memory loss and painful headaches disappeared, his grades improved, and he even outperformed me in the exams we had later. When we met again after five years, he testified that he had succeeded in his studies and even made it to the university by the grace and power of God. This happened when his university visited mine for some sports games.

On that day, I was greatly encouraged and excited to realize that God could work through an ordinary person like me, just as he worked with Peter, Paul, and other figures in the Bible. I vividly remember sensing the power of God coursing through my body and spirit. My blood felt electrified, and I felt a bubbling sensation of God's power within me.

From that time, a new world opened for me, it was the world that is never seen by the physical eye, nor can it be explained by human understanding and philosophies that if one could hear about it without experiencing it, may think it is impractical. The Word of God became so much alive for me as Hebrews 13:8 says, "Jesus Christ is the same yesterday today and forever" (NIV).

I held the belief that the miraculous events recorded in the Bible could still occur today through Jesus, Who remains unchanged. With this understanding, I began to perceive the spiritual realm more vividly, as this fresh world unfolded before me.

A Sensitive Spirit

As I was walking later that day, I encountered another friend of mine, and I sensed a dark spiritual presence surrounding him. This friend of mine had attended our prayer meetings before, but for the first time, I felt this dark energy so strongly around him. I asked if I could assist him, as I believed he needed help to receive the freedom he deserved as a child of God.

I informed him of my desire to pray for him, which he agreed, and we decided to meet that evening. When the time arrived, I prayed for him, and the presence of God was overwhelming. He began to tremble vigorously, and like the demons who spoke out when confronted by Jesus, I witnessed the same, all by the power of Jesus right before my eyes. As Mark 16:17 says, "And these signs will accompany those who believe: in my name they will drive out demons" (NIV).

I used the power and authority granted to me in Jesus's name to command any spirits that were causing my friend to be in bondage to leave him. I was able to drive the demons out of his life, and he was finally freed from their hold. Following the prayer, he experienced a surge of joy in his heart and was noticeably happy. He also expressed a pristine sense of peace that he had not felt before. This experience had a significant impact on his faith, as he encountered the life-changing power of God in real time, and his belief was strengthened as a result.

Later, he proceeded to share with me that he had been aware of a problem in his life but was unable to identify it. He mentioned that following the prayer, he felt a sense of relief as if a weight had been lifted off his spirit.

I am aware that there exist numerous teachings and beliefs concerning demons or unclean spirits, some of which are quite intricate and challenging to grasp. Nonetheless, I strive to read and comprehend the Word of God in its simplicity, and I put it into practice. By doing so, I find that even the most complex ideas become more straightforward and practical.

Since this day, the spirit of God surged through me. It was as if a lifelong dream had finally come true. I found myself ministering the Word of God and offering prayers to my fellow students almost every weekend, which in turn strengthened me even more. At that time, I had advanced to form three, the equivalent of eleventh grade, and was about sixteen years old.

While at home, I ministered at youth gatherings held in my local church. There were occasions when I was entrusted with leading the main service, and every time I ministered, the presence of God was strong. As more testimonies emerged, the presence of God became even more intense. I was sometimes invited to preach at various Christian gatherings, and each time I stood to minister, I could sense the power of God covering me, and the Holy Spirit would give me the courage to boldly proclaim the Word of God.

It is apparent that at times, God expects us to take the first step of faith before He takes care of the rest. Prior to this experience, I was unaware that the qualities I had admired in others, such as the way in which God worked through them in the Bible and in modern times, were present within me until I took a step of faith to release and apply them.

I would like to take this opportunity to encourage all those who are searching for their purpose in life or striving to accomplish a lifelong goal, particularly young people who are aware that they possess something extraordinary within them that could transform their world for the glory of God, to take action and make a difference.

This could involve starting a business, excelling in school, or utilizing the skills and talents bestowed upon you by God to create an impact. You will be amazed by the wonders that God can work when you take a leap of faith and step forward. You are never too young to make a difference and be used by God in any endeavor, just check this out: "Josiah was eight years old when he became king, and he reigned in Jerusalem thirty-one years. His mother's name was Jedidah daughter of Adaiah; she was from Bozkath" (2 Kings 22:1 NIV).

Josiah was eight years old when he was entrusted with the leadership position for a whole nation, and as you read through, you will discover how in his reign, he changed the whole country as he followed the guidance of God.

If you're reading this book and you think you're old and not a youth anymore, you might feel like it's too late, and there's nothing you can do. But I want to assure you that God can use anyone who is willing to step out in faith. Take the first step and start representing the kingdom of God in the area you feel He has gifted you in.

Abraham was already one hundred years old when God finally fulfilled His promise and purpose in his life (Genesis 21:5). This shows that age doesn't matter when it comes to being used by God. You might be the answer to someone's prayer today, so don't hesitate to step out and let God use you. Making the decision to help others can bring contentment to your heart and make you a solution for someone as you represent God to them.

As I served more, my spirit became more alive, and I gained a deeper understanding of God and His ways. I no longer felt unqualified before God, but rather, I felt qualified by His love and grace. This shift allowed God to work wonders through my life. I was able to touch other people, and every time a miracle occurred, it drew me closer to Him and helped someone else draw closer to God.

Once, I visited a particular church where some of my school friends attended. During the service, there was a girl who suffered from a strange ailment. From time to time, she would experience a complete paralysis from her waist to her feet, rendering her unable to stand or walk. Unfortunately, this happened again while she was in church. She was lifted up to the front for the pastor to pray for her, but I watched as she cried in agony without any change in her condition. I was filled with sadness, but there was nothing I could do as I believed it was beyond my jurisdiction. Once the service concluded, I returned to school with my friends.

Subsequently, my school organized a joint prayer meeting with another school, which happened to be the same school the girl with the strange disease attended. During the meeting, I led the prayers, and the presence of God was palpable, so much so that I could physically sense its weight. After the service, the girl's friends brought her to me and explained her condition. I was taken aback to hear of another bizarre occurrence that afflicted her. They revealed that at times, when she slept, there would be bloodstains on her pillow or bedding, but there was no trace of blood on her body.

Filled with the power of God, I stretched my hand over her, and her legs started vibrating as she cried. I commanded every fowl spirit behind her problem to leave her and finally she lay on the ground. I told her to stand up and she walked peacefully from there. From that day, the problem ceased. She sent me messages after some time, expressing how she was very thankful, and I gave glory to God.

To conclude this chapter, I want to share another testimony. While leading the morning devotions for SCOM at my school, one of our fellow students had a problem with his eyes. He often experienced severe pain and sometimes had difficulty seeing. Despite waking up with eye pain on that day, he still attended the morning prayer session.

As I stood in front teaching the Word of God and leading prayers, he suddenly felt a cool wind blowing into his face. It was a bit warm and calm, with a beautiful sunrise from clear blue skies, and there was no wind blowing outside. Since we were inside a classroom, it was surprising to hear that he felt wind blowing into his face.

When the wind disappeared, his eye problem vanished with it, and he was very happy because of how quickly it happened. He was amazed at how the Holy Spirit had worked out the miracle. This is how God began to work wonders and, in the process, opening my spiritual eyes to see more of Him and His power, and what happened afterward will even blow your mind.

CHAPTER 3

A Demon That Came in the Form of a Human

As mentioned previously, I had the responsibility of leading morning devotions. On one beautiful Saturday morning, the sun had just risen, and the environment was serene, with a gentle waft outside. We gathered in one of the classrooms and commenced our prayers in the presence of God, as was our custom.

I opened my Bible and began to read from the book of Ephesians, chapter 6, to my fellow students. As we read, I spoke about the importance of fighting against spiritual darkness rather than against flesh and blood, as stated in that chapter.

It's worth noting that the school we were attending had a well-fortified fence, and only one entry gate was guarded by security personnel who scrutinized visitors before granting them access. This security measure ensured that only authorized individuals were permitted to enter the premises. Even parents or guardians were restricted from visiting during the school term, with only one or two designated visitation days scheduled for the entire term.

While I was encouraging my friends, something strange occurred. Through the window, I noticed a tall, dark-skinned man approaching the classroom we were in. He had an air of determination, appearing somewhat deranged and yet, an intent on finding his targets.

He was wearing what appeared to be a headdress made of animal hide that encircled his head. He had on a black suit that wasn't particularly well-tailored, and there was a ragged hole at the back of his jacket. In his hand, he held a black bag.

As the man approached our classroom, I noticed the guard following him from a distance and crouching behind another building. It was clear that the guard was afraid of the man, so he didn't try to stop him or reach out to him. This was concerning since the guard was supposed to protect the school and its students from dangerous situations. As a result, I felt a sense of dread as the man continued to move closer and closer to our classroom.

The man appeared incredibly threatening, and a few students claimed to have spotted a knife in the black bag he clutched. Even though I was leading the other students in prayer and had taught about having faith and being fearless, I was absolutely terrified. I had never faced such a menacing situation before. Sometimes, it's easy to be bold and confident when preaching the word, but when faced with negative reality, we can quickly forget everything we've learned. And that's precisely what happened to me on that day.

As he got closer, I quickly scanned the classroom to see which window was open and easily accessible in case this man had any intentions of harming us. In Malawi, most buildings have burglar bars, but our classrooms didn't have any. This was an advantage for me because I could jump out and escape if needed. All these thoughts were running through my head at that moment.

The man came closer than before and reached the only door of our classroom where we were praying and fellowshipping in the presence of the almighty God. He attempted to enter the room forcefully, but something unexpected occurred.

It was like he had glimpsed into the abyss of hell beyond the door, causing him to recoil and retreat, unable to cross the threshold of the classroom. From a distance, the guard observed but made no attempt to intervene, amplifying the fear of the situation. The man didn't move from the door, leaving me in a constant state of unease. I was grateful he didn't enter but still kept a wary eye on the nearest window in case things took a turn for the worse.

We froze in place, wondering what this stranger would do next as he loomed over us in the doorway. Abruptly, he began speaking, yelling at us in our mother tongue, uttering the words "kumangopempherapemphera basi," which meant he was bored with our usual prayers and never liked them, with a face twisted in fury. None of us had ever encountered this man before; it was inconceivable that someone like him would be able to enter our school.

After the man spoke in our native language, he started speaking in a language that no one understood. The language sounded like some kind of strange and sinister dialect. He continued speaking in these tongues for a while and then gruffly left. I felt a wave of relief wash over me as he departed, but my mind was still reeling from what had just happened. I knew that this man was not like any other person I had encountered before, based on his appearance and the strange energy he brought with him. After he left, there was no mention of him from anyone on campus, and we never saw him again.

Mystery Unfolded

One Saturday evening, after I had finished ministering to my fellow students, the Holy Spirit led me to the adjacent classroom. Once there, He instructed me to speak with one of the students, Joseph, who was hanging out with his friends. I didn't know him personally, but I knew him from a distance as he had not been involved with any of the prayer meetings and was two classes behind me.

I reached out to him and shared the word of knowledge that the Holy Spirit had revealed to me. I encouraged him that he had a God-given gift that could bless others if he began to use it. Joseph received my message with joy, and we became good friends. Over time, he began to attend our prayer meetings and minister to fellow students. Together, we grew in our faith and supported one another in various ways.

One weekend evening after one of our usual SCOM meetings, a classmate of mine, Yohane (not his real name), who wasn't much into prayer, attended the meeting and later found me. He confided in me that something was wrong and that he felt a strong need for me to pray for him.

I asked Joseph to join me in prayer. As we prayed, evil spirits began to manifest. We were able to cast out most of them in the name of Jesus, but there was one demon that refused to leave. It was strange because it started saying personal and private things that no one could have known. It talked about my life, my family, and other details that seemed to suggest it had been following me for a long time.

It wasn't just me that the demon had information on, it also had knowledge about Joseph's life and family, as well as Yohane's circles. It was as if the demon knew almost everything about us, which was overwhelming and scary. After questioning it for almost an hour, I was frightened by how much personal information it had on each of us. This was something I never expected.

Out of curiosity, I asked the demon who it was. To my surprise, the evil spirit spoke the same language that the strange man at the door had spoken. The demon then revealed that it was the second in command to the devil. I cannot say for certain whether this was true or not, but based on my experience, it certainly seemed possible.

The demon then started describing the day the strange man came to our classroom and gave us a meticulous account of everything that happened. The evil spirit claimed that it had been sent to attack us physically, but its mission failed. The demon detailed all of its actions that day and how it had attempted to destroy us physically because it had been unable to do so in the spiritual realm for a long time despite numerous attempts. The person we were praying for had not been present during the previous morning devotion, but the evil spirit spoke about everything that had happened that day, and all the pieces fit together perfectly. It was a demon that had taken on human form.

We prayed for Yohane, and he was delivered from the evil spirit. It was as if he was reborn. He had believed in God before but then, he felt something supernatural had happened to him. He had a problem with his eyes and used to wear glasses, but after the evil spirit left him, he was instantly healed. This doesn't unequivocally mean that wearing glasses is a sign of demonic presence in a person. Although that may be true in some cases, it is also normal in nature and can happen to anyone.

The demon spoke about how it caused his face to become covered in sores, making him look old and unattractive. After just two weeks of being transformed by the power of God, all the sores on his face were completely healed, and he looked much smarter and younger. As a result of the freedom he got, he started performing better in school and even outperformed me in the subsequent exams. But more importantly, he developed a stronger relationship with God than ever before.

Yohane and I became very close friends after his encounter with the liberating power of Jesus Christ. Our passion for God grew even stronger and we were joined by three more friends (Emmanuel, Andrew, and Ernest) who shared the same fervor. Despite being in different classes, we spent a lot of time together, sharing meals, praying together, and doing many other things as a group. Together, we witnessed even more miracles and blessings from God.

The wonderful thing is that God began to fill each one of us with the Holy Spirit to the extent that Yohane and Joseph began to flow in the power of God as well and almost every weekend we prayed for people together demonstrating God's power in the name of Jesus Christ.

At first, it looked like a terrible thing when a demon came in human form to fight us physically. But it ended up being a turning point for me to break through even more. There's always a lesson to learn in every situation, whether it's good or bad. It's important to thank God regardless. Sometimes, you won't understand God's will right away, but eventually, it will become clear. You don't have to stress out trying to figure it out. Even when you don't understand anything, you can still trust God. He's always in control and overseeing everything.

CHAPTER 4

Supernatural Signs in the Heaven above and on Earth Below (Part 1)

In the last days, God says, "I will pour out my Spirit on all people. Your sons and daughters will prophesy, your young men will see visions, your old men will dream dreams… I will show wonders in the heaven above and signs on the earth below" (Acts 2:17, 19 NIV).

Minding about the last days has become a cliché to many Christians, and even nonbelievers. Many of us are desensitized to the idea that the end of time could be near, and we are primarily focused on accumulating wealth and comfort in our lives. We think that the worst thing that could happen to us is losing what we have worked hard for, rather than being concerned about our eternal destiny.

We are called to pay attention to the signs of the times and be prepared for the second coming of Christ. The end of time should not be taken lightly or as a distant event, but as a reality that could happen at any moment. The following are some of the signs that Jesus said would appear in the last days and we hear their fulfillment every day: "There will be great earthquakes, famines and pestilences in various places, and fearful events and great signs from heaven" (Luke 21:11 NIV).

Let me assure you, as you read this book with full confidence, that the truth of Jesus's return is more real than ever before. Despite the fact that we may only hear from some people from far away,

I have witnessed many signs that I believe attest to His imminent return, and my friends can attest to these things as well.

The Infrequent Sight

Let me explain how everything started. I previously mentioned my friend Yohane, how we became close friends, and how God filled him with His spirit and wisdom. At the time, we were in our final year of high school, and everything was going well. However, on a particular weekday, something out of the ordinary happened.

The day started like any other, with classes and activities going on as usual. In the afternoon around 3:00 p.m., something strange happened. The atmosphere outside seemed different, and everything felt off. It was as if time had frozen, and everything was unnervingly calm. There was no wind, and the trees remained still. The sky was partly cloudy, and the sun was hidden behind the clouds.

I had a feeling that something was off and my spirit sensed that things were not normal. I shared my thoughts with my friends, and they all concurred that something was indeed amiss, but we couldn't put our finger on what exactly it was. Deep down, I had a hunch that this was connected to me and my friends in some way.

As I looked up at the sky, something was different. And then I saw it. The clouds. They were frozen in time, as if a photograph had captured them midmovement. Not a single leaf rustled in the stillness. The environment had been transformed into something otherworldly.

For the first time in my life, I experienced something unfamiliar, yet everyone appeared completely unaffected, leaving me bewildered that nobody else noticed the same. As a result, I only discussed it with my friends and kept it to myself otherwise. It's important to remember that sometimes people around you may not see what you see, but that God reveals what he intends to show to the right people at the appropriate time.

As night approached, the clouds remained motionless in the same shape for hours, as if frozen in time. The only indication of movement was due to the rotation of the Earth, but there was no visible change or motion. As it got darker, our ability to observe the clouds further diminished.

The Obscurity Unpacks

After finishing my evening routine, it was time for our daily prayer meetings at SCOM. The prayer meetings were held for thirty minutes after supper before our mandatory lone study time. I joined my friends in our usual classroom, and other students came as usual to pray. As I was the one leading the program, I stood in front.

As the short prayer service was ending, I noticed Yohane in the back and realized he was behaving abnormally. From my position in the front, it was clear that something was wrong. I suspected a spiritual attack and became fearful because there were less than fifteen minutes until night studies began. At our school, everyone was required to be in their classes studying during this time. If we were found praying instead of studying, we could face disciplinary action, including suspension or expulsion. Our school was very strict, and if we were seen as disturbing studies, the authorities could even ban daily prayers on campus.

When someone was under a spiritual attack, it would usually take at least thirty minutes of prayer to command any unclean spirits to leave them in the name of Jesus. During this prayer, I would stretch out my hand and command the demons to leave. When doing so, I could feel a strong energy coming out of my hand like electricity and then hit the person with force, even if I didn't physically touch the person I was praying for.

As I concluded the prayer service, I heard Joseph's urgent call coming from the back. Being the one everyone looked up to in that place, I knew I had to solve the problem. With my past experiences in casting out various demons, I was confident I could handle whatever was going on. But time was not on my side, and I had to act fast before we got in trouble for praying during study time. Meanwhile, the owners of the classroom were slowly making their way in as the other students left for their respective classrooms. The atmosphere was thick with tension and anticipation.

I charged forward with all my might, fueled by spiritual anger against the malicious spirit that threatened our faith. Placing my hand on Yohane's head, I commanded fire from heaven with the full authority in Jesus's name. However, to my dismay, nothing seemed to change as he stared back at me.

This was not the typical scenario I had encountered before. It felt as though all the energy I had was bouncing off a solid wall. Despite trying every method I knew to cast out the evil spirit, nothing seemed to work. Suddenly, I was hit on my rib side—the spirit had attacked me through my friend. I tried once more but was struck on the other side. Fear took hold of me, and I took a step back to try and make sense of what was happening.

A little shiver ran down my body as the spirit possessing my friend suddenly spoke to me in our native language. The voice was ominous as it uttered the words, "Afana mukamamva satana uja ndine ndikuphani," which roughly translated to "Hey, kid, when you hear of Satan, it's me and I will kill you." I was flabbergasted as I tried to process what was happening. What did he want from us? I braced myself for what might come next, feeling like I had just stepped into a horror movie.

I was fearful that I had to run outside of the classroom to process quickly. It was the first time I had to leave a person who needed my help, as well as my other friends, behind in the classroom. With the clock ticking, the fifteen-minute operation had now become a matter of less than ten minutes.

After leaving the classroom, I ran to a secluded spot under a tree in the darkness, where I lay face-down on the grass and implored God to guide us through the challenging situation we faced. After about two minutes of prayer, I stood up, and within a minute, I heard my friends calling my name. As I made my way back to them, Joseph informed me that Yohane had been calling out to me, requesting that I pray for him.

Upon hearing that, a glimmer of hope flickered inside me because, at least, he was back to himself a bit. Still, my apprehension grew even stronger because I was unsure of what to do. When I finally met Yohane, He asked that I breathe into his mouth. As I did so, it felt like a heavy burden was being placed on him, causing his muscles to tense up, and he suddenly crumpled to the ground. It was only then that he was released from the shackles of Satan that had plagued him.

As he rose, the bell rang, and we quickly made our way back to our respective classes, feeling relieved that we had avoided detection by the school authorities. That night, I was filled with a sense of exhilaration, convinced that I had successfully expelled Satan, the father of all lies. Nevertheless, I realized later that it was not solely my doing. God had intervened, sending His angel to engage in battle against the devil. I will provide a detailed account of the angel in the subsequent chapters.

It was now apparent that the strange sight was not a miracle. On the contrary, we had an unwanted visitor, the devil, in our vicinity.

It's Not Over Yet

We believed that the ordeal was over, but it soon became evident that the battle had just begun. We discovered that the devil attempted to defeat us through various means, including sending a demon in human form, which ultimately failed. Undeterred, the devil then attempted to attack us directly, but once again, he was unsuccessful because of God's protection over us.

I want to emphasize that if you have God on your side, you are safe, and the devil has no power over you. It is my belief that some of the challenges my friends and I faced, were allowed by God to demonstrate His power and sovereignty, and to show that He is greater than any adversary. I hope that this message will inspire and encourage you to put your faith in God, knowing that He is able to overcome any obstacle.

"What, then, shall we say in response to this? If God is for us, who can be against us?" (Romans 8:31 NIV).

Despite all his failed attempts, the devil continued to send spiritual attacks. This is a common characteristic of Satan, as he never gives up, no matter how many defeats he suffers. It is important to remember that Satan has been losing since the beginning, and his ultimate defeat is inevitable. I am certain that the challenges we faced during this period were permitted by God for a specific reason.

When I refer to spiritual attacks, I am referring to the malevolent forces that would target individuals in my vicinity, leading me to engage in prayer circles to fend them off. At times, I experienced spiritual attacks that had a tangible effect on me, manifesting as a sensation akin to being swarmed by rats upon entering a room. Although I could not see anything in the physical realm, I was acutely aware of the attack due to the unsettling feeling it evoked.

The constant praying circles to ward off evil spirits became tedious, and we were at a loss for what to do. It was an exhausting ordeal. I reached a point of desperation and made the mistake of asking a particular demon while casting it out, for advice on how to stop the attacks once and for all. It's important to note that demons are skilled in deception, and it's crucial to be guided by the Holy Spirit to discern truth in any conversation with them. In fact, it's best to avoid such conversations altogether.

Surprisingly, the evil spirit we had questioned suggested that my friends and I should observe a twenty-five-day fast to end the attacks. The answer appeared spiritual, but my guess is that it was a ploy by the evil spirit to keep us in a perpetual cycle of spiritual battles, knowing fully well that it would be a daunting task for six students to endure such a long fast, causing us to grow weary.

I had never fasted for even fourteen days by then and I knew it would be a challenge. But we were so desperate that we would do anything to be free. We accepted the challenge and agreed to start fasting the next day.

Remember, by this time, I could sometimes see things that were going to happen before they happened as I prayed. The same thing happened before we started fasting. I told my friends that God was going to manifest signs physically and my friends are witnesses to this. In the second part of this chapter, I will explain the details of this.

CHAPTER 5

Supernatural Signs in the Heaven above and on Earth Below (Part 2)

We started fasting the first day. Typically, when students opted to fast, whether as a group or individually, they would congregate at a spot within the campus to pray. During lunchtime, while other students went to the school dining hall to have their meals, the prayer area usually remained unobstructed. As was customary, my friends and I went to pray during lunchtime while observing our fast. While praying, I received a message in my spirit which I conveyed to my friends, as it felt like it had erupted from within me. My friends were present and can attest to it.

The message was "I hear a thunder in the kingdom of darkness now." As soon as I uttered these words, we all heard an actual thunder, and I believe it was a validation of the message. We were all astounded, including myself, by what God had manifested in that instant since it was my first time encountering such a phenomenon. It was the first physical wonder that happened during this period.

We broke the fast together in the evening. During the night of that day, I was sitting with my companions on the hostel veranda, having a chat.

As we conversed, I saw a vision. It was my first real time vision in the spirit realm.

I saw a massive hand surrounded by light, with a bright, glowing finger writing in the sky. I immediately shared the experience with my friends, and astonishingly, letters resembling Hebrew characters started appearing in the clouds. These letters were not tiny, but rather substantial in size, making it apparent that they were meant solely for us to perceive. It was a sign that God was with us and had wonderful plans for us. This event motivated us and provided us with encouragement for the following day of fasting. We were eagerly looking forward to abstaining from food for several hours of the day.

On the second day of our fast, we returned to our customary prayer location during lunch while other students were having their meals. While praying, I saw another vision in which I could see what seemed to be a hedge of fire descending gradually from the heavens. The vision felt extremely vivid and realistic.

As the hedge of fire drew nearer, I sensed an increasingly intense presence. I shared my vision with my friends as we continued to pray. Suddenly, I found myself saying, "God is here, God is here." At that moment, one of my companions appeared to lose control of his faculties as the Spirit of God filled him. It was as though an intense force had overpowered him, causing his muscles to contract uncontrollably, leading to him shaking and ultimately falling to the ground.

The events that followed will be forever etched in my memory. We all fell face down as God spoke through my friend, proclaiming the words, "I Am Who I Am." The atmosphere was filled with nervous anticipation and excitement. It was a surreal moment, as the same God who appeared to Moses in the burning bush (Exodus 3:14) had descended to be with a group of teens from the outskirts of one of the less known countries in the world.

The atmosphere changed completely. My spirit was completely in tune with the presence of God, and I felt that the Creator was there with us. During this time, God spoke many things that were personal to almost everyone present, expressing His deep love for us. He also spoke about our past, present, and what was coming next in our lives, including events that would follow from that moment. It was a profound experience for me and my friends as we encountered the presence of the living God.

After the experience with God, He promised to protect us from any of the spiritual attacks and assured us that there were thousands of angels surrounding us. It was difficult for me to understand why a powerful God would send so many angels to protect a group of young and inexperienced individuals like us. I'm sure some people might also question why this was necessary. Others might even doubt the whole experience because we weren't in positions of great importance or influence in society. However, I believe that God's love for His children knows no bounds, and His protection extends to all of us, regardless of our station in life.

God's love for you is immense, and He is deeply concerned about you. Sometimes, the battles you face in life are there to show you how much He is with you and how He has surrounded you with His angels. Even the smallest details in your life are important to Him, as seen by the fact that He numbers the hairs on your head (Matthew 10:26). You may feel insignificant and think that you don't matter much to society or those around you, but God sees you as His precious vessel. In His eyes, you are a big thing about to happen. You have a purpose and a plan that God has designed specifically for you, and He wants you to trust in Him to lead you to it. Remember that no matter how small you feel, God's love and concern for you is vast and never-ending.

I understood later why God had put such a defense around us as I witnessed spiritual battles in the heavens, behind the unseen world, that involved thousands of demons waging war because of us.

On that day, God spoke directly to us and warned us about the persecution that we were about to face at school. He told us that every step we took would be closely followed, but also reassured us that we would overcome it all. At the time, I didn't fully understand the gravity of the message, but soon enough, the persecution began. It was one of the toughest times in my life, as we faced opposition not only from our peers but also from the school administration. In the chapters to come, I will expound the details of the persecution we faced and how we were able to overcome it through God's help.

A World of God's Messengers

In the evening, my friends and I gathered in the hostel to break our fast. From that day, I felt a shift. The unseen world revealed itself to me in a new and powerful way. I started seeing more personal visions and a whole new world of angels opened up to us. Whenever God wanted to communicate with us as a group, He would send an angel to speak with us in the same way that He communicated with us on the second day of our fast. These experiences were always profound and had a lasting impact on us. Through these encounters with angels, we were given the opportunity to have a real-time, up-close experience with the unseen world as a group.

As we spent time together after breaking our fast, an angel descended and spoke to us in almost the same way God descended and communicated to us. He said that we no longer needed to continue our fasting, as God had promised that the spiritual attacks would no longer trouble us. With those words, a great weight was lifted off our shoulders, and we were filled with the peace and joy of the Holy Spirit, as the attacks vanished.

We received yet another surprise when we learned that God had sent Angel Michael to be with us, and on that day, he spoke to us. We knew it was him because he introduced himself by name. From that moment on, he became like a friend to us as a group, and we enjoyed asking him many questions and learning from him. In the upcoming chapters, I will share more about the things we discovered through our conversations with Angel Michael.

After our encounter with Angel Michael, my friends and I were hesitant to share our experience with anyone. We knew that people often think of Michael as a protector of nations rather than individuals, and many see him as a serious and constant warrior in the spiritual realm. We were afraid that if we told anyone about our encounter, they might dismiss us as crazy or delusional. We kept our experience to ourselves and continued to learn from Michael and the other angels he introduced us to.

It wasn't until about a year later that I came across the ancient book of Enoch. As I read through the pages, I was amazed to find that the book described Michael and the other angels in much the same way as we had experienced them. I knew from my spirit that our experience was authentic as it drew us closer to God, but I was even more upbeat to know that our encounter was not a hallucination or a figment of our imagination, but rather a real and profound spiritual experience.

I started learning from angels, not only for my spiritual life but also for my social and academic life. This was a turning point in my life as everything changed. My perspective on many things changed, and in the next section, I will share some of the lessons that I learned and still apply today.

That day marked the end of our fasting and we spent more time sharing the gospel with other students and demonstrating the power of God.

Joseph and Yohane were also filled with the Holy Spirit that we ministered the gospel together and our ministration was accompanied by different signs and wonders.

Signs in the Heavens

There was an instance where I was chatting with my friends in the hostel during our leisure time. Suddenly, I received a clear message from an angel in the spiritual realm. This angel held a special place in my heart because he helped me in my faith and offered guidance on leading a simpler life. The angel instructed me to rush outside and follow his directions as he led me. I obediently followed and he guided me to the administration offices which were located approximately 328 feet (100 meters) away from the hostels.

Upon my arrival, the angel instructed me to look upward, and to my amazement, the sky was filled with stars and the moon. Above me, high in the sky, there were words arranged in a straight line, which appeared to be meticulously crafted. Although I did not recognize the language in which the words were written, they resembled Hebrew letters to me. It also crossed my mind that the language might be unique to heaven, as there are various languages and forms of writing in the heavenly realm. The experience was particularly meaningful to me since it brought back a cherished childhood dream that I had recurrently experienced.

In the dream, words would emerge in the sky. The words were typically love, kindness, patience, hope, and peace; and they were written in English. Each time I had this dream, it felt like I was experiencing a glimpse of heaven—it was a sweet and wondrous experience. Now, during this encounter as a teenager, it was as though this dream from my childhood had come to life before my eyes. The following image is not the real image of the words I saw but gives a very close picture of what I saw that night:

As I beheld those words in the sky, I felt an overwhelming sense of joy and wonder. They then slowly began to fade away until they disappeared completely, and I made my way back to the hostel. I want to emphasize that I witnessed this amazing occurrence with my own physical eyes, not through a spiritual vision or a dream. Although I may not fully understand the meaning of those words, or whether they were from my childhood dreams in another language, I firmly believe that God orchestrated this experience to allow me to share my testimony in this book and confirm the scriptural prophecy of signs appearing in the heavens during the last days. As you continue to read, you will discover that God revealed many awe-inspiring wonders in the skies that left us in complete awe.

On another occasion, while walking with my friends Joseph and Emmanuel from the hostels to our classes, we engaged in conversation, minding our own business. As we were approaching the classroom area, we suddenly heard Angel Michael instructing us to gaze upward at the sky.

To my great surprise and joy, what I beheld in the sky was beyond my comprehension. As I gazed upward, I saw the letters of my first name, "Kelliote," and the first letter of Joseph's first name forming in the sky with magnificent clarity and size. The letters were a brilliant white against the backdrop of a sky that was an intense shade of blue, illuminated by the late afternoon sun. The following image is not the real picture of that day but gives a close idea of what we saw:

As I looked up at the sky, it was evident that the letters *J* and *K* stood boldly next to each other. Within a mere minute, the *K* began to transform, gradually taking on the shape of an *E*—a nod to our friend Emmanuel who was with us. Inquisitive, I asked Angel Michael about who was responsible for these magnificent writings in the sky. Michael explained that the writings were being crafted by angels, with the exception of the time when I had a vision of a gigantic finger writing in the sky. In that instance, the writings materialized in physical form because it was the finger of God.

One may question why God would show such immense interest in the lives of teenagers like myself and my friends, considering our young age (I was sixteen while Joseph and Emmanuel were around fourteen years old). I, too, have often wondered the same thing, asking myself, "Why me?" However, what I have come to understand is that this is simply how God operates with His people. His love is boundless, and He chooses to reveal Himself to us in extraordinary ways, regardless of our age or position in life. It is a testament to His unending grace and mercy, and a reminder that we are all valued and cherished by Him. In His eyes, no one is too insignificant to be the recipient of His love and grace.

Most of these occurrences take place in the unseen world every day. You might not witness signs in the sky, hear an angel's voice, or encounter anything extraordinary, but God is always working behind the scenes with unconditional love for you, just the way you are. At times, I wonder if one of the reasons why God allowed us to witness these signs was so that they could be documented in this book, ensuring that everyone knows the God who created the universe is still alive and knows us by our names.

On another occasion, I had a vision of being in heaven where I saw countless strong angels dressed like soldiers marching. Interestingly, Joseph had a similar experience during his own alone time, where he also saw the same vision of angels dressed like soldiers marching in heaven. We were both surprised and amazed by this revelation, and we discussed the details of our experiences. In later chapters, I will dive into the specifics of what I saw in that vision.

Days later, as Joseph and I chatted outside one of the junior classes, the Holy Spirit was with us, and we were engrossed in our conversation.

Then, out of nowhere, we heard an unexpected sound of thunderous marching in the sky, as if an army was approaching, with each step heard as a distinct "left, right, left, right." The sound was so powerful that it felt like it was shaking the very ground we were standing on.

We felt that they were somehow connected to what was happening in our lives at that time. The sound surprised me, so I asked the Holy Spirit for an explanation of what was happening. I was stunned when He revealed that the thunders were the actual sound of angels marching. According to the Holy Spirit, Angel Michael had asked God to let us hear the sound as a confirmation of the vision we had seen earlier so that we could believe that it was real. Even now, I am still amazed by this experience, and the memories are still vivid in my mind.

More Wonders

One day, while I was completely rapt in studying, I suddenly noticed a peculiar phenomenon occurring before my eyes. Out of nowhere, a bright, shining object resembling a small star suddenly emerged from my eyes and bounced off my exercise book. The object was so radiant and dazzling that it immediately caught my attention. The light emanating from it was white-blue, and it seemed to glow with an otherworldly intensity. As it landed on my notebook, it lingered there for a few brief moments before vanishing just as suddenly as it had appeared. This strange occurrence left me feeling bewildered and amazed, wondering what it could possibly mean.

I do not know what it was, and how in the world would such an object fall from eyes without me even feeling it. The image below is not the real picture, but it can give you a close idea of what it looked like:

On another occasion, I was chatting with a friend when I witnessed the same incident where a light star fell from my eyes, then onto my nose and vanished. Similar to the previous occurrence, I cannot comprehend what it was, but I believed it could be a celestial indication. It's possible that it was a grain of sand from heaven, but I don't know how it entered my eyes since I never sensed it. I recall a comparable star-shaped object falling on my physical science exam paper during my senior high school national exams, and I had a strong feeling that I would pass that paper.

Another time, I was at home in my bedroom late at night when I heard a sound like that of a local drum outside. I opened the window to listen more carefully, in case there was something unusual happening in our enclosed compound. However, to my surprise, the sound was coming from the sky, and it was as though someone was playing a thunder drum. I couldn't help but burst into laughter as I heard the sound because I knew it was a supernatural sign for me to hear. It was quite amusing to imagine someone playing drums in the sky at such a late hour.

Similarly, there was a time when I was at school and for nearly an hour, there was a continuous thundering sound coming from behind the clouds, like the unceasing noise of a waterfall. It was truly remarkable. I recognized these occurrences as signs from above meant to bolster my faith, and the faith of those who heard it, as well as those who would later hear the testimony.

One day, I sat down with my two friends Emmanuel and Joseph as we chatted different stories and behold a sign appeared in the heavens above. It was an image of a horse running with a rider on it. It was a well-crafted image with the clouds; angels are like the best artists. This was not just a pattern observed in the clouds. The sky was blue and on top of us was that image. The image below is not the real picture, but it can give you a close idea of what it looked like:

While I may not fully understand the significance behind it, the experience of seeing the image was truly awe-inspiring. I knew deep down that it was a sign from above, fulfilling the prophecy that in the last days there shall be signs in the heavens above.

Signs of the Combat

Once, Joseph and I were privileged to witness a spiritual battle between the angels of God and evil spirits as imagery in the sky. It's known that the kingdom of darkness wages spiritual battles over the children of God from time to time, and in response, God sends His angels to fight on our behalf. These battles occur behind the veil of the unseen world, but Joseph and I were fortunate enough to witness one of these battles in the physical realm, as the angels were displayed in bright white clouds with various forms while the demons were in dark clouds.

The clouds we saw were not ordinary, they moved at incredible speed and in different directions, forming various shapes in the sky. We were the only ones who noticed because Angel Michael had informed us about the spiritual battle taking place. Such battles occur frequently in the unseen world, waged by the forces of darkness against the children of God, and God sends his angels to fight for us. We were astonished to learn that this battle was happening because of us, though we had no idea why. This made us understand why God had promised to surround us with thousands of angels, it was an army.

Behind the unseen world, God is constantly fighting for us, as we patiently hold our peace in faith, as Exodus 14:14 reminds us. During this battle, Michael directed my attention to a large cloud that had taken the shape of a lion's head with an open mouth. He explained that this was a symbol of the lion of the tribe of Judah, and that the cloud represented his presence. Although Michael himself was not the lion of the tribe of Judah, he explained that when the angels fight, they do so under the authority of Jesus Christ. The lion's head on the cloud was a representation of this divine authority.

The white and dark clouds were moving in various directions, colliding with one another, with the exception of Angel Michael's cloud. When I asked him why he wasn't fighting and engaging like the other angels, he explained that the war had not escalated to a challenging level, and he only intervenes when things become exceptionally difficult. This resonated with the following scripture: "But the prince of the Persian kingdom resisted me twenty-one days. Then Michael, one of the chief princes, came to help me, because I was detained there with the king of Persia" (Daniel 10:13 NIV).

I then asked him why he was still there when he was doing nothing as the fight was going on, and he answered plainly that he just wanted to show himself to us. The chief archangel just came for us. Thus, how much God loves His children including you and me because I know Angel Michael was just a messenger of God.

After showing himself to us, Angel Michael said that he was leaving the battlefield. As soon as he said the words, "I am leaving," the large cloud that had been motionless began to retract from the battlefield, moving slowly. Its grandeur was splendid compared to the smaller and faster, moving clouds in the field. It was an incredible sight to behold Michael, the "big brother," in that scene.

Some may wonder how one angel could be with us and at the same time be in the battle place. The answer is that angels are not omnipresent, but they can be in more than one place at a time as they have the power to do so.

On another occasion, we were getting ready to attend a joint prayer meeting with different schools under SCOM. We were aware that such gatherings often provoked spiritual battles against the strongholds of those places. It seemed that wherever we went to spread the gospel, we were inviting a spiritual battle between light and darkness.

We prayed for that meeting that God should give us victory and that His angels would fight for us. When we were about to go to that school, I was together with Joseph. Michael was also there in the spirit, and he said to me, "I went to monitor the place and the stronghold is so small and I can't be part of that fight, other angels will deal with them." He then said, "I am coming back, and you will see a sign on top of you."

After looking in the sky for about a minute, a large cloud came into view and quickly moved very close to us. As it passed by, Michael exclaimed, "That's me!" I don't mean to suggest that angels are clouds but, rather, that God used symbols and representations to teach us. I believe these signs are a part of what God said would occur in the last days, and it's become increasingly apparent that Jesus's return is drawing nearer.

These are all true sayings worthy to be believed and reflect on our lives and make a choice to begin standing up strong for Christ. The saying that Christ is coming is as close now like never before, and it is high time we make strong and unshakable decisions to follow Christ.

To conclude this chapter, I want to share with you some significant events. During one of our regular daily prayer meetings, I was leading the prayers in our usual classroom when a blackout occurred, which was not an uncommon event as we experienced it several times a week. However, something out of the ordinary happened while we were all praying in the dark.

There was a physical lightning that struck within the classroom. It wasn't coming from outside but right inside the room, and many others witnessed it. Later on, a fellow student who was also my friend approached me and asked if I had seen the lightning while we were praying. On another occasion, I was with my close friends in a hostel, and we experienced two separate lightning strikes in front of us. They happened in between beds, at two different times on the same day.

These are just a few examples of the signs and occurrences that took place during that period. There were many others that left me in awe and reinforced my belief in a world beyond what we can see with our eyes. These experiences also helped many people come to believe in Jesus Christ. Some of our teachers even joined us for our prayer sessions.

On one occasion, a student who was a Muslim approached me and my friends and expressed a desire to receive what we had. We welcomed him and shared the Word of God with him, and he eventually became a believer. The amazing thing was that we prayed for him, and he was filled with the Holy Spirit as he fell to the ground and prayed. The joy and jubilation on his face could not be hidden.

The majority of those who attended our prayer gatherings were filled with the Holy Spirit. Joseph, Yohane, and I were able to show the power of God almost every weekend, proving the existence of the invisible world to others. We commanded arms to instantly grow, and they grew. Many times, as we ministered, people would be overcome with uncontainable joy and laughter as they experienced the love of God poured out into their hearts. You would hear uncontrollable giggles all over the place. We spoke in tongues and interpreted them, often revealing accurate words of knowledge to others.

There were times when I could see an angel in the spirit standing, and I could instruct someone else to stand in the same spot. However, they would either fall or be pushed back when they tried to do so. These experiences were a clear indication of the reality of the Kingdom of God, which has always been overt.

When riding a vehicle, I could see angels flying at the speed of the vehicle right outside it. Many times, I could see angels standing maybe in our home or walking with some other random people. My spiritual eyes were just open and sensitive as God allowed it to happen. This is just the normal behind the unseen world even though we might not see it with our physical eye. Our part is to trust in God and rest assured in His love.

My purpose for documenting all these signs is to serve as a living testimony to the fulfillment of scriptures and to strengthen your belief that Jesus is alive and indeed coming again. You can share these experiences with others and introduce them to Jesus who has the power to save their lives. Initially, I was perplexed as to why God exposed me to so many supernatural signs that often made no sense and were unexpected. I now realize that it was for this exact reason—so that I may share these experiences with the world. When God revealed all these things to me, He had you, the reader of this book, in mind because of His love for you.

CHAPTER 6

An Account of the Ministering Spirits

> Are not all angels ministering spirits sent to serve those who will inherit salvation? (Hebrews 1:14)

> "The angel of the LORD encamps around those who fear him, and he delivers them." (Psalm 34:7 NIV)

Recall when I shared about God's incredible promise to send His angels to accompany me and my friends? The reality is that God sends His angels to watch over and protect His righteous ones, just as it says in the opening verse. If you are a child of God, then you can be confident that the angels of God are with you. While some may question or reject this truth, it doesn't change the fact that God has indeed sent His angels to be with His beloved righteous ones. So let's embrace this promise and take comfort in the divine protection and guidance that we have as the sons and daughters of God.

Angels are dispatched as ministering spirits to those who have embraced the salvation offered by the living God. It's crucial to keep in mind that every encounter with angels should center around God, whether we're aware of it or not. I'm bringing this up because some individuals have become fixated on the notion of experiencing angelic encounters, leading them to lose sight of their primary focus on faith in God.

Experiences with angels or other supernatural phenomena ought to bolster our faith in Jesus and deepen our connection with God. Any experience that diverts our attention away from God must be carefully examined. This is how we discern whether an encounter is genuinely from God; any supernatural occurrence that elevates itself above God is not of divine origin. An experience from God should illuminate His kingdom and fortify our bond with Him.

The purpose of this account is to heighten our awareness of the spiritual realm that lies beyond the physical world perceptible to our eyes but discernable to our spirits through faith. It highlights how much God works behind the scenes on our behalf, affirming our conviction that "we serve a living God." Our understanding of the unseen realm is intended to broaden our perspective on our beliefs, strengthening our faith and deepening our experience of God in that respect.

A Class with Angel Michael

God's angels had been a topic of fascination for me for quite some time. Through my reading of the Bible, I discovered that God has worked wondrous miracles through angels, and I had heard of numerous individuals with extraordinary encounters involving these celestial beings. However, despite my belief that God dispatches angels to protect His children, I never imagined such an experience would happen to me.

Before encountering angels, I underestimated their influence in a person's life. Although God sends His angels for our welfare, we may find ourselves in difficult situations that could have been avoided had we been aware of what God has for us.

As I had previously mentioned, the very first angel that I had ever experienced was Michael. I speak of this angel more frequently than any other because he is the one that God had allowed me to connect with the most. Michael and I interacted so often that most of the lessons that I will share in this chapter were imparted by him. It was truly fascinating because I had always regarded him as a distant being that I could only read about in the Bible, but suddenly I was able to communicate with him directly.

What made my experience with Michael remarkable was the fact that he frequently reminded me of his presence. Every time he did so, a sense of inner peace and confidence filled my heart. It was reassuring to know that he was always with me, watching over me, and ensuring my safety.

I was in awe of the fact that I had a personal connection with an angel that was believed to be only involved in protecting nations, not individuals. It seemed impossible, yet there he was, with me and my friends. As I wrote this book, I couldn't help but notice that this angel was watching me intently and occasionally nudging me with reminders of events from my teenage years. It was an incredible experience that left me feeling both humbled and stunned.

During my conversations with Michael, I was thrilled to hear him say that angels are very fond of people and cherish every moment they get to interact with us. He explained that every time God allows them to communicate with us or manifest themselves in any way, they are filled with joy and enthusiasm. I could sense his excitement as he conveyed this message to me, and it made me appreciate the joy of being one big family of the children of God. Knowing that they are happy to be with us reinforces the fact that we are not alone in this world and that God has assigned angels to be our helpers and protectors.

God does not require angels to protect or guide people; He can do it independently. Similarly, God does not depend on anyone to accomplish His goals, but instead, invites everyone to establish a relationship with Him and serve Him. Serving God is an act of worship toward Him. Likewise, angels' service toward God is also an act of worship. That's why we strive to do everything for God's glory. Just as we feel complete in the presence of God, angels also feel complete as they serve Him.

Even if you don't have the opportunity for direct communication with your angels, it's important to remember that they love you deeply and are always willing to carry out God's will on your behalf. They often send messages and signs to guide you on your path. Don't hesitate to speak to them, even if you don't receive a direct response. Your angels are always watching over you and may even be smiling at you from beyond.

Angel Michael was more than just a spirit being to me; he was my friend. God had allowed us to form a deep connection, and Michael had always demonstrated his willingness to serve God as he loves people like me. And the same is true for any other angel that God has assigned to watch over you. We once had a funny moment when we joked about his age, considering he has been around for thousands of years. He had a great sense of humor and replied, "I am very old!"

Through observing Michael in our interactions, I gained insight into his deep humility and unwavering love for God, which surpasses anything else. Michael himself confided in me about having been in God's presence for thousands of years according to our time, yet he has never fully comprehended the vastness of God. This underscores the enormity of the divine mystery, with our limited human understanding merely scratching the surface. It is truly a privilege to have any knowledge of God that He has revealed to us. Like any other angel, Michael holds God in the highest regard and carries out His commands even when it is beyond his understanding. Despite Michael's immense power and size, he gladly serves people as God instructs with great joy.

As the angel was speaking to me, he told me that he is the angel who always defends the name of the Lord. He went on to explain how in the beginning Satan was cast down out of heaven.

He said that God is always seated on His throne, and He does not leave it. Even when there are stories of how God came down to earth, it is His presence that comes down, not Him leaving His throne in heaven. God is always present on His throne, ruling with majesty and sovereignty.

The following verse resonated with this: "But you, LORD, sit enthroned forever; your renown endures through all generations" (Psalms 102:12 NIV).

However, there was a time when God wanted to take action against Satan, who was once the leader of all angels but desired to be on the throne of God. God was extremely angry with Satan's arrogance and disobedience, and He wanted to fight him Himself.

At this point, Michael the angel asked God if he could be the one to fight Satan with the other angels on God's side. God granted permission, and Michael and the angels fought against Satan. Michael described how, during the battle, he delivered a powerful kick that hurled Satan down to earth like a bolt of lightning. This event is an example of how God's angels are always ready to defend His name and carry out His will, even in the face of powerful opposition. I find the following scripture relatable to what he said: "And there was war in heaven. Michael and his angels fought against the dragon, and the dragon and his angels fought back. But he was not strong enough, and they lost their place in heaven" (Revelation 12:7–8 NIV).

Angel Michael and the devil have been great rivals since that time. He told me how much he despises the devil, and his hatred for him only fueled my own. He eagerly awaits the day when we will strike a huge blow against the devil. He spoke of a time when the devil will be bound and held captive, and even believers will have a hand in striking him.

Angel Michael spoke of this day with great excitement, eagerly anticipating the moment when he can deliver a powerful blow to the devil while he is bound.

The immense love that the angel has for God is quite evident. Most people are familiar with the story of the walls of Jericho crumbling down, as recounted in the book of Joshua in the Bible. Angel Michael shared with me his role in that event, revealing that he was the mysterious figure that Joshua encountered and asked if he was a friend or foe.

This time, he appeared as a man. He told me it was one angel who destroyed the wall of Jericho, and it was him. I was very fascinated when he told me that and I went back to crosscheck in the Bible. The details were very fascinating, everything made more sense to me.

> Now when Joshua was near Jericho, he looked up and saw a man standing in front of

> him with a drawn sword in his hand. Joshua went up to him and asked, "Are you for us or for our enemies?"
>
> "Neither," he replied, "but as commander of the army of the LORD I have now come." Then Joshua fell facedown to the ground in reverence, and asked him, "What message does my Lord have for his servant?" (Joshua 5:13–14 NIV)

According to Michael, angels can take on human form sometimes when God sends them on a mission, as we see in the passage mentioned earlier. He also mentioned that whenever they get the opportunity to interact with people, they feel joyous about it. I suggest reading Joshua 5–6 for more fascinating insights into the story.

He once asked me, "Have you ever wondered why demons always look filthy while angels are always beautiful, even though they are angels who rebelled?" I pondered the question for a while but couldn't come up with a satisfactory answer. I replied with uncertainty, and he proceeded to explain that demons' appearance is a result of the punishment inflicted upon them by the angels of God. They are constantly beaten and burned, which is why they look so unclean.

It is quite baffling to me why people often discuss more of demons and their supposed powers rather than focusing on the superior power of angels from God's side. Throughout history, whenever there has been a confrontation between angels and demons, the demons have always been the ones to retreat and suffer defeat. Michael once shared with me an important piece of wisdom that has stayed with me to this day. He said, "Remember, CHILDREN OF GOD NEVER LOSE." This statement has given me the courage and strength to face any challenge in life, knowing that I have the backing of a powerful and victorious force on my side.

The protection that God has granted you is so secure that there's no need to fear anything in this world. All evils come from the devil, but God has implemented measures to keep him forever subdued. Fear is one of the devil's weapons, as it makes it difficult to trust in

God, and faith is what pleases God. Therefore, be vigilant against the devil's attempts to scare you with the various situations in your life. Refuse to give in to fear and always remember that children of God never lose.

It's important to remember that as a believer, you have the support of God and all of heaven behind you. No matter what may be happening in your life, God is always aware and watching over you. Even when things seem confusing or difficult, you can trust that God has a plan and is working everything out for your good.

Sometimes it may feel like the devil has gained the upper hand and is trying to bring you down, but you can take comfort in knowing that God is in control and has already won the ultimate victory. It's important to resist the devil's attempts to fill you with fear and doubt and instead hold onto your faith in God's promises.

And when it seems like everything is taking too long or that your situation is hopeless, remember that God operates in His own time and that His timing is perfect. You can trust that at the right time, He will bring about your victory and fulfill His promises to you.

In addition to this encouragement, Angel Michael taught another valuable lesson that we will explore further.

Everyone Is Tested

There have been moments when I needed help from the angels assigned to me, but I couldn't seem to receive it. There were times when I wanted to prove my faith to others so much that I wished for an angel to perform something supernatural for them to see with their own eyes.

However, it never happened. So I asked Michael why this was the case since the angels were sent to be with us. He answered simply, stating that they only act according to God's will. He then shared with me his experience of being with Jesus during His forty days of fasting and temptation in the wilderness. As angels, they simply watched and did not intervene as the devil tempted Him.

Michael also mentioned that there may be times when God permits the devil to test us, and during such times, angels do not have the power to prevent it. Instead, they watch over us to ensure that everything goes smoothly and that we are not harmed. I was surprised when I later came across a scripture in the Bible that supported Michael's example of angels being present during Jesus's temptation in the wilderness: "Jesus said to him, 'Away from me, Satan! For it is written: Worship the Lord your God, and serve him only.' Then the devil left him, and angels came and attended him" (Matthew 4:10–11 NIV).

After Jesus was tempted by the devil in the wilderness, the angels came and attended to Him. It made sense to me why the devil asked Jesus to throw himself down so that the angels could catch him. He must have seen them watching. This example reverberated something to me because sometimes I find myself in situations that I feel I should not be in, given how much God has put standards over my life, including the presence of angels. Yet I have come to understand that it is always God's will, and His will is perfect for me. I have learned that even in those challenging situations, God is working things out for my good, and I often discover miracles later on.

As I reflect on my past, one of the most distressing moments I can recall happened in the year 2016. It was a couple of years after I received these profound teachings from God's angels, and I was only nineteen and in my first year of college. Throughout my life, I had experienced malaria several times, but I usually recovered in a matter of three days after taking medication. Nevertheless, this time, it was different. The malaria I contracted was the severest form I had ever experienced, and most of the medications prescribed to me had no effect. The disease attacked my red blood cells, and as the medication failed to work, I began to deteriorate. I lost an alarming amount of weight in a short time, and I found myself frequently admitted to the hospital, receiving treatment through intravenous drips.

Despite taking another prescription from a different hospital, my condition didn't improve; I just got a short relief. Still, I returned to school hoping to recover gradually. However, my condition deteriorated, and I frequently felt like I was blacking out. I had to fight to remain conscious until one night, I was eventually rushed to the main hospital in the city in the university emergency vehicle, to receive treatment from the best doctors.

The doctor who examined me there spoke to my parents and me, warning us that he would be giving me the final treatment for malaria. He also told us that if it failed to work, it would be the end as there was nothing they could do. Despite my fear, I agreed to the treatment. But instead of improving, it felt like the medication was attacking my body, causing other complications to arise. I felt helpless and unsure of what would happen next, as my life hung in the balance.

When I was feeling hopeless due to my illness and my prayers didn't seem to be working, I decided to call upon Angel Michael for help. He had previously taught me how to call upon him in an emergency and he had come to my aid a few times before. However, he had emphasized that this was to be kept strictly confidential and not to be shared with anyone.

I prayed, and then I called Angel Michael for help. I was in my room at home when suddenly he appeared in the spirit realm with a great display of power and energy. The whole room was filled with a tangible sense of tingling electricity that even my body could feel. He spoke just two words: "Don't worry."

Despite this incredible encounter with the angel of God, I remained frustrated and disappointed that nothing seemed to change in my physical state.

After delivering those comforting words, the angel left. However, I couldn't find much comfort in them because all I desired was an immediate healing. Eventually, by the grace of God, I started to recover gradually over time, and I was spared from death even for a second.

I learned the lesson through difficult experiences. Although I had been instructed on it before, I never truly comprehended it until I went through it myself. Enduring trials can seem like a trite phrase until it becomes a tangible reality. It became apparent that angels solely carry out God's plans. There will be moments where we will face challenges, but these struggles will not defeat us because; despite appearing to be abandoned, God is still present and watching over us.

I gained the insight that God alone is sovereign and is a respecter of no man. It's essential to remain humble and acknowledge Him as the source of all blessings. I captured the following photo at my college hospital when I was diagnosed with a severe form of malaria. Despite my weak pulse, I smiled, trusting that God would heal me, and I knew that I would look back on this experience and see that God had delivered me. However, as time passed and my recovery took longer than anticipated, my smile faded, and I became frustrated; yet this situation built me.

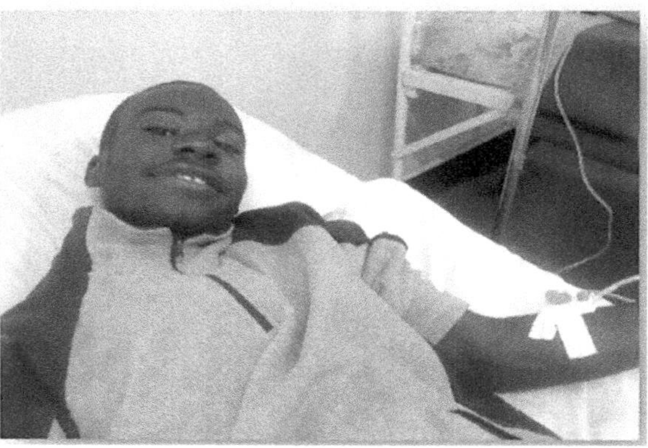

On one particular instance, the devil himself came to fight against us. This occurred after many unsuccessful attempts through his agents. When he appeared, his method of attack was to target someone that either myself or my friends were praying for, or someone close to us, similar to how Yohane was attacked, as I mentioned earlier. Sometimes I imagine this is how Satan entered Peter as well to try frustrating the plans of Jesus: "Jesus turned and said to Peter, 'Get behind me, Satan! You are a stumbling block to me; you do not have in mind the concerns of God, but merely human concerns'" (Mathew 16:23).

It was a challenging moment when Satan attacked us again, and my friend Joseph and I attempted to call Michael to help us fight.

Unfortunately, on this occasion, he did not show up to assist us. Instead, he told me later that he and the other angels were watching from afar.

We were left to face the struggle alone, relying on the knowledge of the scriptures and the lessons we had learned from the angels about warfare.

After a difficult struggle, we finally managed to defeat the stubborn devil. Later on, while chatting with Joseph and some other friends, Angel Michael showed up in the spirit realm and congratulated us on becoming stronger and more spiritually capable. He explained that we had faced a great challenge and had overcome it. It's important to remember that even though it may feel like God has abandoned us when we don't receive immediate backup, in reality, God may be building us up for greatness.

Angelic Duties

God assigns different duties to angels, with some, like Michael, designated as fighters while others are appointed to fulfill various roles in our lives. It came as a surprise to me when I learned that an angel had been helping me with my budget sometimes without my knowledge.

It's common for us to take the communication of angels for our own thoughts as we cannot easily tell the difference. Sometimes, the ideas that occur to us are actually messages from the angels that God has appointed to be our guardians. Beyond protection from harm, these celestial beings have been tasked with aiding us in living a life of physical and financial health, fostering positive relationships at all levels, providing guidance in ministry and aiding us in making important decisions.

As I share these thoughts, some may wonder if angels encroach upon the responsibilities of the Holy Spirit. The answer is quite simple: they work in harmony. Personally, I have experienced the Holy Spirit as a close, great, and even best friend with whom I can confide in and receive guidance from, beyond just prayer. I also worship Him because He is the Spirit of God. This is why I have come to truly love God, and the God I know is not merely what I've heard of but a living reality.

I have experienced different duties of angels in my life, and most of the times, I might not know but angels are giving in ideas and instructions big time and the same applies to every other Christian.

During a time of fellowship with my friends, Michael introduced us to another important angel—Raphael. Until then, I was only familiar with Gabriel and my other angelic friend. Raphael's name was new to me, and it wasn't until I read the ancient book of Enoch four years later that I discovered stories about this angel, which confirmed what I had been told.

I like this particular angel as he possesses a calm and collected demeanor, unlike Michael who tends to be quite loquacious whenever God grants him the opportunity to communicate with individuals like myself. It's worth noting that Michael greatly enjoys socializing and occasionally indulges in humorous banter. In fact, he once confided in me that angels often find amusement in observing our solitary behavior and the comical actions we engage in when we believe no one is observing us.

There was a moment when Angel Michael recalled a memory to me that amused the angels. I had invited some friends over to my place, and we had set out some food on the table. I noticed that there was an even tastier dish in the kitchen, but there wasn't enough of it to share with all my guests. So I quickly consumed the dish in the kitchen, thinking that no one had noticed. However, during our later conversation, the angel reminded me of this incident, and I realized that I had been mistaken in thinking that I was alone and unnoticed in the kitchen.

Returning to the topic at hand, I became acquainted with Angel Raphael, and although our conversations were not extensive, I appreciated his wise words. To this day, I admire his ability to impart wisdom. Through his advices, my life has been enriched with practical philosophies that I continue to live by. He guided me in approaching various situations with simplicity, whether it was regarding my academic pursuits, social interactions, or spiritual journey.

The quote that has had a profound impact on my life is "Do what you are supposed to do, don't force yourself." While this statement may seem simple at first glance, its true meaning and significance became clear to me through the advices of Angel Raphael who gave me those words. His guidance led to a series of revelations and insights that helped me live a life free from undue pressure.

Since adopting this approach, those who are close to me have noticed that I have a strong aversion to working under pressure. I have learned to prioritize my responsibilities and execute them in a deliberate and focused manner. This has allowed me to stay on track without feeling overwhelmed or stressed out.

Whenever I encounter a shocking or unexpected situation, I remind myself to relax. This is because Angel Raphael used to tell me "relax," and the word had power to calm my nerves. As a result, I am able to approach these situations with a clear mind and a sense of calm. Some of the people closest to me have observed that I frequently use the word "relax," but may not understand the reason behind it. However, they will gain a deeper understanding of its significance upon reading this book.

Angel Raphael made me understand clearly that God is never caught off guard by anything that happens in our lives. This insight has helped me to avoid unnecessary stress and anxiety. Instead of worrying about the unknown, I trust in God's divine plan and His ultimate purpose for my life. By doing so, I am able to approach each day with a sense of peace and calm.

This lesson was so impactful that I decided to include it, along with many other pieces of wisdom that I have gained in my book titled *Christian Wisdom and Philosophy in 1000 Proverbs*. The book was first published in 2020 and serves as a testament to the profound impact that realities behind the unseen world have had on my life.

Both Raphael and Michael provided invaluable assistance with my academic pursuits. Despite many people close to me assuming I was not putting in effort, I excelled in my academics. While some attributed my success to innate intelligence, I knew that my accomplishments were the result of divine intervention.

I want to emphasize that my experiences were unique to me and were ultimately for the glory of God. I caution against attempting to replicate my journey without first seeking God's guidance. Instead, I encourage everyone to work diligently without succumbing to unnecessary pressure.

There was a time I really needed to study very hard so that I could pass the exams that were coming ahead. Now let me give you a brief background of how the school system works in Malawi.

There are six renowned public universities in Malawi. These institutions provide excellent education at an affordable cost, making it possible for students from low-income families to continue their studies. However, admission to these universities is highly competitive and based solely on performance in the form 4 (grade 12) exam.

Every year, thousands of students in their final year of high school sit for the same national exam which determines whether they will be able to attend one of the six top public universities in Malawi. Due to the limited number of available spots, competition is fierce. The exam is overseen by government-appointed invigilators and the Malawi police to prevent cheating. Only the most intelligent and diligent students make the cut and are able to fulfill their dream of attending one of these prestigious universities. For many students, their parents, teachers, and other concerned parties, this is the ultimate goal.

The success of a secondary school is measured by how many students it sends to the top 6 universities. This exam is the deciding factor for every student's future and career, which makes it incredibly serious. I was in the same position and had to work extremely hard to be among the top students. Coming from a low-income family, even the affordable public university was a concern for my parents, and they could only hope for the best.

I was eager to put in the hard work, but to my amazement, the duo of Michael and Raphael intervened and instructed me to divert my attention to jotting down the proverbs for my book, which I mentioned earlier, or to delve into studying the Bible instead. Although I attempted to reason with them, they remained resolute in their stance. Whenever I attempted to study against their directive, they would use force to stop me.

To clarify, when I said "stopped me by force," I mean that I was physically disturbed until I put away my exercise books. I experienced a burning sensation within me, which was very troubling and difficult to describe. It was a new and unfamiliar sensation in my body, and at first, I thought Michael was lightly hitting me. However, he later explained that he was just blowing air on me because if he hit me, I would die.

This was an exciting experience for me because most of the instructions I received were in the spiritual realm, but their effects could be felt in the physical world.

I found it difficult to endure the sensation of the blowing and had to comply with their request in order for it to cease. As a result, my studying was frequently interrupted, causing me to make little progress.

When I hadn't yet met these angels, I used to continue studying after regular class hours, but when Team Michael and Raphael came into my life, they instructed me to stop studying beyond class hours and I followed their advice. It was a big change for me because I used to be the only high school senior who did not take my studies seriously.

In 2014, I was supposed to take the Malawi School Certificate of Education (MSCE) exam, which is the final national exam that determines a student's educational future in Malawi. The exam is notoriously difficult, and most students know that achieving good grades requires intense studying. During this period, students often sacrifice sleep to study as much as possible. Many students who do not usually pray become serious with God, hoping for divine intervention to improve their chances of success. Teachers also intensify their teaching to prepare students for the rigorous exam.

For me, however, things were different. Despite the importance of the MSCE exam, I was not studying as much as I should have been. It was a stressful time, knowing that I needed to perform well on this exam to secure my future, yet Angel Raphael calmed me with his words "Relax!" and all the stress melted away.

I continued to live my life in that manner, focusing on praying, studying the Bible, and sharing the Word of God with others, all while allowing the Holy Spirit to guide me in manifesting God's wonders. Nonetheless, as the time for the national exams approached, I began to feel the weight of reality and sense knocking at my door. I was suddenly struck with fear that I had not studied enough for the exams that would determine my future.

Again, despite my fears, Raphael would remind me to "relax" on a daily basis, and his words had a powerful effect on me. Whenever he spoke those words, my fear and stress would dissipate, although it would sometimes creep back in, and I had to maintain my faith and trust in what God had done in my life during that period.

One day, the day before my national exams, I entertained the thought of studying hard and extending my hours of study, hoping that Team Michael and Raphael would understand my situation. I hoped they would grant me a last-minute miracle in those hours. It was the final exam, and I knew I had to put in the extra effort, just like every other student.

I was confident that I could convince them, so I planned to study for longer hours. I usually studied for one hour and thirty minutes every day, from 7:00 p.m. to 8:30 p.m., but I wanted to extend my study hours. As soon as I was about to start, I heard a loud and clear voice of an angel telling me to "Go and sleep!" It felt like I had awakened sleeping giants.

I expressed my objection and reasoned to myself that they couldn't comprehend that it was exam time. I also thought about what people would think if I failed the exam since everyone, including my teachers and peers (as I will recount in the upcoming chapters), knew me as the preacher man and the Jesus freak.

I rationalized with myself and convinced myself that extending my study time was the right thing to do. Within a minute of starting, I was physically agitated by the angels again. I felt like a harsh wind was blowing inside me, and the sensation was overwhelming this time. I hastily packed my things and ran to my hostel while laughing because it felt like the angels were teasing me. Although uncomfortable, it was a fun experience.

Immediately, I left the place we were studying in, he stopped disturbing me, and I made a commitment to myself that I would just study my normal hours during all the exam time and that is exactly what I did until the end of the exam.

As the exam approached, something incredible happened. In the last few hours of preparation, I suddenly gained a complete understanding of the entire syllabus. At one point, I tried to practice math problems, but an angel instructed me to simply read the math material instead.

This went against the advice of teachers and conventional wisdom, but I trusted the angel and followed the guidance. The end result was astounding—I ended up receiving a distinction in mathematics, one of my best performances.

I successfully passed all eight subjects of the exam with very good grades, and as a result, I was selected to attend one of the top public universities in Malawi. At the time, when I first wrote this book in 2018, I was pursuing my BA in agri-economics at that university.

Despite being in college, I still heard that familiar voice urging me not to work hard. I had become so accustomed to it that I didn't bother to argue. Whenever I heard it, I simply obeyed without question. One time, during my second year, I was required to take a course from the engineering department, and there was a mid-semester exam approaching. This course was notoriously difficult and was taken by around four hundred students from various programs. In the days leading up to the exam, everyone was frantically studying and trying to solve the complex engineering math problems. Despite feeling scared, I attempted to prepare for the exam, but then I clearly heard the voice saying, "Don't touch anything for this exam, just go and write!"

I felt grateful and relieved when I heard the instruction, thinking that I would be saved. My confidence was shattered when I saw the exam paper. The toughest question I had feared would come was right there in front of me. It was worth a substantial twenty-five marks out of the total of forty. The other two to three questions combined were only worth the remaining fifteen marks, and I only knew how to answer one question, which was worth less than ten marks.

In that moment, I felt utterly betrayed and hastily scribbled down whatever came to mind just to avoid leaving any question blank, as per my rule. Unfortunately, my efforts were in vain, and I anxiously awaited my exam results. When they finally came, I was devastated to see that I had scored only 12.5 percent of the total marks available. However, to my astonishment, the lecturer announced that there was an error in the last question, and everyone was to receive free marks for it. This meant that my score jumped up to 75 percent.

I was aware that there were things happening in the unseen world, and it was possible that they were related to me. Perhaps I was being guided to understand events before they occurred. It's amazing how much simpler life becomes when we follow God's instructions. It's worth considering how many times we've ignored those quiet, inner voices only to realize later that we should have listened. These voices may be our angels offering guidance and assisting us in living a simple and comfortable life.

Although I wasn't the brightest student in my college class, I managed to secure a scholarship to study abroad before any of my classmates. In 2020, during the COVID year, I was offered an online master of business administration in data science program at one of the top private Indian universities. The program was sponsored by the Indian Ministry of Foreign Affairs. The following year, I was given another opportunity to study in the United States, and as I wrote the second version of my book in 2023, I was studying there.

I have shared my testimony not for my own sake, but to glorify God and to let you know that His angels are present to guide you even in your academic pursuits. You may not encounter them in the same way I did, but they are there, offering inspiration and direction to your thoughts. Follow the lead of your spirit and focus on the ideas that bring you peace and motivation.

Other Angels

I encountered several other angels during my spiritual journey, including Angel Gabriel, although I did not interact with them extensively. My encounter with Angel Gabriel was unique, as I had previously heard stories of people being afraid after meeting him, but he approached me in a very friendly manner. Every time he came, he announced, "I stand before God and always bring good news." Whenever Angel Gabriel communicated to me, I felt joyful even before he spoke because I anticipated that something positive would occur—and it always did.

Michael sometimes delivered bad news, such as warning me about potential upcoming problems, but he would always follow up with encouragement on how I would overcome them. It was comforting to have this heads-up, even though the news itself may not have been good.

On the contrary, Gabriel always comes with good news, and I enjoy asking him questions and receiving his guidance. He has shared many humorous moments with me, and although I have several personal testimonies about him, I might not share all of them in this book.

However, I will include at least one.

One time, the sky had frozen, and the clouds stood still. As I mentioned earlier, it was apparent that the devil had come to our school once more. But this time, I didn't pay him any attention. This time, I knew he was foolish and powerless, and as the Bible states, he roams around like a roaring lion, seeking someone to devour (1 Peter 5:8). He only scares those who are afraid and panicked, making them vulnerable to his attacks. If you trust in Jesus and his finished work on the cross and are not afraid of the devil's power and activities, he has no hold over you.

I was aware of his presence at our school, but I didn't pay much attention to him. However, I still felt uneasy, not because I was afraid of him, but because I knew he could cause trouble for me through others or by other means. To be honest, I was more afraid of the school administration than I was of Satan. This lack of peace in my heart made me think, "When will Satan strike so that I can fight back in Jesus's name?"

I did not encounter any physical trouble during that time, but I came to understand later that Satan only came to tempt us because God allowed him to do so. It's important to know that God may permit the devil to test you at times, so don't lose hope when it seems like Satan has a hold on you. Remember the story of Job in the Bible and have faith in God. If you're not familiar with the book of Job, I encourage you to read it for yourself and you will be fascinated.

I cannot be certain if the devil attempted to tempt me and my companions, but I am certain that he did not succeed. It is a common misconception that the devil appears as a serpent when he tempts you.

In reality, he infiltrates your mind, just as angels communicate with your thoughts. Though he may have tried to test me through my thoughts, I was unaware of his attempts, and I never succumbed to his temptations.

Despite this, I remained uneasy because the clouds remained frozen until the following morning, indicating that the devil was still present. At around 10:00 a.m., Angel Gabriel spoke to us and delivered the news that the devil had descended the previous day but had since been vanquished and was departing. As he spoke, the clouds began to move once again, and the sky was filled with motion.

I was surprised when Michael introduced me to another angel, and what he said next may come as a surprise to you too. He revealed that there are female angels, a concept that had never occurred to me before, leaving me quite astonished. Michael went on to explain that there are even female major angels, and he mentioned one called Parisha who is a warrior angel. Although I didn't have much interaction with her, I thought it was interesting to learn about her existence.

Another time, Angel Michael informed me about a group of angels whose role is to fight with fire. One Sunday morning, a major fire angel came to me and informed me that he would be accompanying me throughout the day. As he stayed by my side, I began to feel my body temperature rise and my skin becoming very hot, even noticing the heat in my breath. In spite of this, I did not experience any weakness, sickness, or pain. On the contrary, I felt very refreshed. I even asked my friend Emmanuel to touch my skin and feel the unusual heat, which he did. This angel serves as a commander to other fire angels, and their primary task is to engage in battles with fire.

On another occasion, Angel Michael informed my friends and me that there were angels stationed high in the sky above us known as "angels of the tower." He explained that these angels functioned similarly to the watchmen in ancient city walls, who could spot any incoming attacks from a distance. Similarly, the angels of the tower watched over us in the spiritual realm and communicated with the angels assigned to us, preparing them to defend and protect us as cherished children of God.

As a sign, he explained that sometimes the sky would open up right above the location where the angels are positioned, which was precisely any location I was at. Even if the entire sky was covered in clouds, the area where the tower angels were present would have a clear, blue opening. This opening seemed to follow me no matter how far I moved from one position to another. This has allowed me to bask in the warmth of the sun on an otherwise cloudy day, a privilege I cherish.

As I reflect on my experiences with angels, I am convinced that they are real, and that God has indeed sent them to us by his grace. I have come to understand that there is nothing that can take me by surprise, for God knows everything and has his angels watching over me. My encounters with these celestial beings have strengthened my faith in God's love and protection for me, and I am grateful for the reassurance that comes from knowing that I am never alone. As I share my stories, I hope that they will inspire you to believe in the existence of angels and the power of God's grace and to take comfort in the knowledge that you too have his angels on watch over you.

CHAPTER 7

A Glimpse of the Third Heavens

"I know a man in Christ who fourteen years ago was caught up to the third heaven. Whether it was in the body or out of the body I do not know—God knows" (2 Corinthians 12:2 NIV).

In the verse above, Paul talks about how he went to the third heavens and heard inexpressible things. I've recorded that verse because there are individuals who remain skeptical about the possibility of being caught up to heaven and returning alive while still living. Throughout my life, I've been fortunate enough to have several experiences in heaven ever since God granted me a glimpse of it through my spiritual eyes. Although I may not recall all of them, they have left a profound impact on me.

In 2014, I had my initial experience of seeing heaven. Although the vision was not very intricate and happened in a flash, it left me feeling exhilarated because it was the first time I had ever seen heaven.

Interestingly, on that same day, Yohane also had a vision of the same thing, and we were both thrilled to recount the same details.

During my first vision of heaven, I was sitting outside on the veranda of my hostel when I suddenly found myself in a trance-like state. In that moment, a short but powerful vision flashed before my eyes. I saw myself approaching a grand, golden gate, and as I passed through it, I knew immediately that I had entered the gates of heaven.

Although the vision was brief, it left an indelible mark on me. I did not see many details, but the feeling of being in heaven was overwhelming. It was a moment of pure bliss and joy, and I felt as though I had transcended to a higher plane of existence. Even though I had never been to heaven before, the experience felt incredibly real and surreal at the same time. It was, without a doubt, one of the most profound moments of my life.

The feeling that washed over me as I walked down a heavenly street was beyond words; it was pure love and joy, so intense that it's still etched in my memory to this day. The street was nothing like I had ever seen before; it was lined with stones that shimmered like gold, and every step I took filled me with awe and wonder.

As I walked, I couldn't help but marvel at the beauty of the street. The stones looked so much like gold, but I was uncertain if they were genuinely made of the precious metal or not. From my understanding of heaven, I had learned that there was a type of stone there that was incredibly precious and stunningly beautiful. It was said that God had used that stone to create many of the things in heaven. The stone's appearance resembled that of gold, but it was far more valuable than gold could ever be.

I was in complete awe of this experience as it was etched very well in my mind. The experience left me feeling so fulfilled, and I knew without a doubt that it was a glimpse of something greater than myself.

During one of my experiences in heaven, an angel shared with me that many individuals often see the precious stone in heaven as gold due to its striking resemblance. In actuality, gold is considered one of the least valuable stones in heaven. The angel went on to reveal the name of this precious stone to me, but I must refrain from sharing it here as it is a secret that I am not permitted to disclose. The knowledge imparted to me by the angel left me with a sense of wonder and a desire to learn more about the mysteries of heaven.

My first vision of heaven left me longing for more. Though subsequent visions did not come right away, that moment marked the beginning of a time where I would experience extraordinary things in the heavenly realm. I can confidently say that heaven is a reality far beyond anything we know or can perceive with our earthly senses. In this chapter, I will dive into my personal experiences and the teachings shared with me by the angels of God and other heavenly beings. My goal is to shed light on the mysteries of heaven and offer a glimpse into the divine realm.

The Open Eyes

At some point following my initial vision, I had another one that occurred on Tuesday, March 4, 2014, which I made a note of. This time, I was sitting in a lecture theater, learning a specific subject. The teacher was writing notes on the blackboard while we, the students, took down the information. This method of transferring knowledge from teacher to student is a common practice in many schools in Malawi.

While I was taking the notes in class, an angel appeared and flew me to heaven. You might wonder how this happened, and it's challenging to describe in words. Still, I can give you an idea. Sometimes, when I'm going about my daily activities, I feel a force striking my heart like a gust of wind. This presence is recognizable to my body as being from another realm. It's like a signal that connects me to the unseen world.

When I experience this, I feel like I am existing in two worlds at once, and my physical body becomes weak while my spiritual eyes and other senses are heightened. This often causes me to feel like sleeping, and I enter a trance state where I can sometimes see figures or clear pictures. In short, I become entranced.

In a matter of seconds, everything changes, and the vision comes alive. It's a tremendous experience where I can perceive everything around me—the sights, the tastes, the emotions of that realm. My heart beats with a sense of belonging, like I've come back home. In a snap, a whole new world opens up, and I transform to be in tune with this world. Unlike others who claim to leave their body behind, I can still sense my physical form, although it feels distant. I hope this paints a clearer picture of what happens to me during the visions that I'll be describing in this chapter.

Whatever I have explained above, happened while I was in that class, and as my spiritual eyes opened, I saw an angel in white with wings and he flew me with him to heaven.

When I am soaring through the air in a vision, the sensation is unparalleled. It's akin to the thrill one might experience while flying as a human, a feeling I refer to as "flying thrills." For some, this sensation may be similar to that of racing cars, biking, or skateboarding. During this flight, we eventually arrived at an enormous gate which was wide open for us, and we passed through it together. There is a big angel who is like one of the guards on the gate who really loves his job.

As I was in class at the time, I wasn't paying attention to the lesson, and I had rested my face onto my desk due to the intense experience. As mentioned earlier, my body felt weak and my eyes closed, and I was transported to heaven. Oddly enough, nobody seemed to notice what was happening to me. They might have assumed I was tired and resting, which is strange for someone sitting in the front row of a morning class. Remarkably, no one paid any attention to me, not even the teacher at the front of the room.

The moment you step foot into that place, you are instantly transported into a realm of unencumbered freedom, much like a bird soaring through the skies, without a care in the world. Trying to describe the sensation as merely "sweet" would not do it justice, as the feeling transcends words and cannot be adequately captured by language alone. It is more like a state of being where you are transformed into a vessel of sweetness, and every fiber of your being is suffused with pure, unadulterated joy.

The air is thick with an all-encompassing sense of love, even if you have yet to meet anyone. It is as if love were the very oxygen you breathe, filling your lungs with a fragrance that can only be described as divine. In this place, you feel as though you are in the presence of love personified, as if it were a living, breathing entity.

Attempting to convey the profound nature of this experience in human words is an arduous task, for the sensation is simply too profound to describe adequately. Nevertheless, I am honored to share my insights and observations with those who will embark on this journey themselves. Through this book, I hope to provide preparation for those who wish to enter the gates of heaven and experience the indescribable sense of love and peace that awaits them.

It is at this moment that you must release yourself from the grip of fearing death and embrace the passing of a fellow believer with a sense of excitement. It is natural to mourn the loss of loved ones, as even Jesus wept when his friend Lazarus died (John 11:35). However, you should also take comfort in the knowledge that your departed loved ones may not want you to grieve for them, for they have been instantaneously transformed into a state of glorious bliss.

In this new state, they are experiencing a form of love that surpasses anything you could have ever given them in life, breathing it in and living it out with every fiber of their being. While it can be difficult to comprehend the full extent of this transformation, you can take solace in the fact that they are now enveloped in a love so profound that it is beyond the bounds of human experience.

If, for some reason, you are not sure if your destiny is heaven, believe in Jesus Christ today and you will have your place in this place. There is more to gain in believing God than to lose while the opposite is true.

After we passed through the gate, I was immediately led to a magnificent gathering of angels who were engaged in fervent worship of God through music. The sheer magnitude of their numbers was grand, and their angelic voices harmonized in a way that was unlike anything I had ever heard before.

In all my years on earth, I had never encountered such a stunning display of musical worship. The closest comparison I could draw was to a peculiar audio clip I had stumbled upon on YouTube. It featured a group of people practicing their choir performance, only to discover upon replaying the recording that there were inexplicable, otherworldly voices blended with their own. These supernatural notes were beyond anything a human voice could produce, and it was as if they had been added by some unseen force.

You can search "angels caught on tape during church choir practice," and the video has blue background with white light rays, and it is just the audio. It is old and not very clear, and I know not everyone can believe that clip and that is okay, but my spirit recognized it and I love it. If you would like to have a glimpse of music from heaven, go check it out.

The heavenly angels were equipped with a wide array of instruments, some of which were unfamiliar to me, and their celestial symphony was truly breathtaking. Overwhelmed by the beauty of their worship, I humbly joined in and offered my own praises to God.

After this remarkable display, the angel who was guiding me led me to another location, soaring through the air until we reached a place where a stunningly beautiful river flowed. Its waters were crystal clear, and the views that accompanied it were splendid. The heavenly lighting and scenery transformed this river into the most magnificent one I had ever laid eyes on.

As we stood by the river's edge, the angel explained to me that this was the fabled River of Life. Mesmerized by its beauty, I asked the angel if I could touch the water, and he granted my request. As my fingers dipped into the flowing water, it felt no different from any other moving water. However, as I made contact with it, I felt an inexplicable presence or power enter my body, leaving me feeling light and at peace.

Not content with just touching the water, I asked the angel if I could drink from the river. The angel granted my request, and as I drank the water, that same mysterious presence once again entered my body. In that moment, the angel spoke words that filled me with wonder, saying, "Every wound has been healed, and every sin has been forgiven." It was a moment that left me feeling truly blessed.

I still don't fully comprehend the reason why the angel said what he said, but the experience was both peaceful and transformative. Even after the vision ended, I could still feel its effects, and to this day, I remember it vividly.

Next, the angel guided me to a place where the armies of the Lord were assembled. The sight was awesome as there were countless angels present, divided into four distinct groups, each led by a commander. It was more like a heavenly military barracks, filled with what I could only describe as "war angels." These are the very angels who fight for us as children of God. If only we could truly comprehend just how much God has our backs, we would never be consumed by fear in any situation.

The Other Side

While observing the war angels, I noticed the presence of Angel Michael, who came to me looking very tall. The atmosphere had shifted, and it felt like a serious meeting without any room for jokes. I guessed this might be because I found him in his office. He introduced himself, saying, "I am Angel Michael," and instructed me to follow him to where he was going. I obliged and accompanied him as he led me to various other locations.

Angel Michael led me to a large room that appeared to be filled with war attires. He handed me one and said, "It is very hard to be attacked with this attire." Then he took me to another place, which can be best described as a massive warehouse full of fire. He explained to me that this fire was the same fire that comes down every time we call upon it in prayer. He emphasized that when we pray and ask for fire, it is this fire that responds.

This fire is commonly used when people are battling unclean spirits, and it is incredibly powerful. If you find yourself fighting spiritual battles, call upon this fire from heaven in faith, and understand where it comes from. It never runs out as it self-replenishes and is never extinguished.

Sometimes, I imagine that the same fire Elijah called down from heaven to consume the sacrifice he was offering to prove to the prophets of Baal that Jehovah was the true God (1 Kings 18:37–38) is the same fire that we can access and use as a weapon of mass destruction against the kingdom of darkness in the authority of the name of Jesus Christ.

Eventually, he led me to yet another location where I saw what appeared to be various human body parts. Angel Michael explained that these body parts are taken by angels and used to fix people whom God has designated. It could be a seemingly impossible physical issue such as a bone that needs replacing, or the restoration of a damaged body part. Essentially, God may send an angel to perform a miraculous healing.

If it aligns with God's plan, miraculous healings can occur, and I have personally witnessed such healings on numerous occasions. Perhaps you have also seen similar occurrences. It is not uncommon to encounter individuals who had previously suffered from broken bones or damaged organs yet were healed after praying to God or having someone pray for them. Such healings often involve the replacement of the affected body part.

During prayer, some people or body parts may vibrate or shake, as angels are performing the operation in the spiritual realm. While some may doubt the authenticity of these experiences, speaking to those who have experienced miraculous healings may offer a different perspective.

After witnessing all these things, I returned to my normal state but felt an incredible sense of euphoria. Interestingly, my brain was not functioning as usual for a while. It was as if I was a little out of myself. I have become accustomed to this feeling over time because I understand that my physical body cannot fully contain the spiritual experiences that occur during visions of heaven or encounters with God. This altered state can last for several days, although it may not be apparent to others just by looking at me.

The Throne

During the same day, while I was in bed and about to sleep at night, I saw another vision. In that vision, an angel came to me like before. This angel took me to heaven again, and for the first time, we flew in heaven until we reached the throne of God. No one told me it was the throne of the most high God, but as we approached it, I could sense that it was the dwelling place of the Creator of the universe.

When I saw God's throne in heaven, I was struck by its immense size and majesty. It was unlike anything I had ever seen before. It made me realize that when we use words like "big" and "majestic" to describe God, we are actually understating His greatness. As I stood in awe of the throne, I realized that anyone who sees it would naturally be compelled to bow down and worship Him. The experience left me feeling grateful to know such an amazing God who is more real and powerful than we can comprehend.

Words cannot really explain the nature of this God, there is so much mystery about God that neither angels nor humans have come to the complete understanding of who God is, and yet what has been revealed about God over the centuries has been powerful enough to transform generations and change the world in many ways.

There is no high building that can be compared to the throne that God sits on. Surrounding the throne of God and the whole atmosphere in this place were strong sounds of thunders and constant lightnings. There was what looked like smoke of foglike appearance, and it was all over the place and there were many sounds that were all over, sounds and voices of worship to the king of kings.

Initially, describing this experience in human terms may seem like this place is frightening, but once you have experienced it, you will realize how stunning and beautiful it is. Whenever there is a storm with heavy lightning and thunder, it invokes a memory of the ambiance in heaven and brings me great joy. It is hard to convey the true essence of this experience through words alone, but I am certain that one day, you, too, will have the chance to stand before this magnificent throne and worship the King of kings.

Heaven has a multitude of beings who are constantly worshipping God. There are so many of them that we don't even know about some of them—we only hear about the living creatures that are mentioned in the Bible. If you are unfamiliar with the living creatures, I encourage you to read Revelations chapter 4 in the Bible:

> And around the throne, on each side of the throne, are four living creatures, full of eyes in front and behind: the first living creature like a lion, the second living creature like an ox, the third living creature with the face of a man, and the fourth living creature like an eagle in flight. And the four living creatures, each of them with

> six wings, are full of eyes all around and within, and day and night they never cease to say, "Holy, holy, holy, is the Lord God Almighty, who was and is and is to come!" (Revelation 4:6–8 NIV)

These living beings have their own names that we do not know, and because of how they appear, anyone who saw them described them as living creatures. Everything in heaven is living and even if you see a lion or any other animal, it is spiritually alive and knows how to worship God.

Whilst I was in this vision, another vision appeared to me as I was in heaven. In that vision I saw Jesus on the cross.

You might be wondering how I was able to recognize Jesus in heaven. It's incredible how, in heaven, you have an innate ability to recognize things without anyone having to tell you. You can encounter a biblical figure and instantly know their name, even if you're meeting them for the first time. That's how I was able to recognize Jesus in heaven.

I had always heard the saying that Jesus suffered for our sins, but it was something I had become accustomed to without truly comprehending the reality of it. No movie or depiction could accurately portray the extent of Jesus's suffering for us. During my vision, I only caught a glimpse of His face and part of His body, and it was an indescribable horror to behold. His body was covered in deep wounds, and it was too overwhelming to look at for more than a moment. It was from this moment that the prophecy about Jesus in the scriptures by prophet Isaiah became clear to me: "Just as there were many who were appalled at him—his appearance was so disfigured beyond that of any man and his form marred beyond human likeness" (Isaiah 52:14 NIV).

Upon seeing the wounds on Jesus's body, I was deeply moved knowing that He suffered for my salvation and the salvation of the entire world. His wounds were not for His own benefit, but for ours. This vision reminded me of never taking for granted the grace that Jesus gave us through His sacrifice on the cross.

Although some people may view our faith as a waste of time or mere illusion, I am convicted that what we believe in is real and more significant than the world we live in. As you read this, I hope that you too are affirmed in your belief that what we hold onto is a treasure, a reality that is more tangible than anything we experience in this life. It is a truth that transcends belief, for everyone belongs to it regardless of their beliefs.

Upon waking up, I returned to myself and slept.

The Ladder

After some days, I saw another vision, and it was on Sunday March 15, 2014. This is one of the visions that I will never forget as the memory is usually fresh as I always recount it.

After returning from church and having a meal, I decided to rest on my bed in my hostel. As I lay there, I started to feel drowsy and soon found myself in a vision. In this vision, I was climbing a ladder that extended high into the clouds. As I climbed, a powerful voice rumbled and echoed throughout the sky, causing vibrations that felt similar to being in front of a loud bass bin speaker.

The voice was so strong that it sounded like a thunder speaking and it said, "You are favored!"

When this voice was heard in the skies, Angel Raphael appeared, and he told me to fly another way with him. In the spiritual realm, you can have wings and fly like angels.

Later, I discovered that the voice I heard belonged to one of the living creatures. Before this experience, I had held some misconceptions about these creatures based on what I had heard. I used to believe that they were mere animals in heaven, preprogrammed to worship God.

However, my perception was entirely incorrect. These creatures are living beings, full of wisdom and authority within the heavenly government.

Their appearance is truly fascinating, as they are adorned with eyes all over their bodies. During one of my conversations with a living creature, specifically the one with a lion's face whom I consider a friend, he posed an intriguing question to me: "Do you know why we have eyes all over us?" I replied in the negative, and he explained, "It's because we see and know all things." It was a profound statement that emphasized their immense wisdom and knowledge in the heavenly government.

He elucidated to me that they meticulously observe all occurrences in the world and unwaveringly keep a watchful eye over God's children day and night. It is imperative for every child of God to comprehend that they are constantly on His mind.

Despite their intimidating appearance and immense power, one may presume that the living creatures are perilous to approach. I, too, shared the same apprehension until I discovered their profound affection for God's children and their delight in worshipping Jehovah the most high. It is astounding how every living being in heaven exudes love and grace toward God's children. Someday, you will witness these things in heaven, and I am eagerly awaiting your experience of them.

As Raphael and I left the ladder, we flew toward a brilliantly shining location where angels were present, and yet there was no sun. From there, we continued to another area where I could see homes and vehicles. The angel explained that what I saw would become a reality on earth in due course, and he further revealed that whatever we possess on earth is already known in heaven. God has already designed and planned it. Building a house is simply the fulfillment of God's plan. I later discovered that this concept is mentioned in the Bible as well:

> All the days ordained for me were written in your book before one of them came to be. (Psalms 139:16 NIV)

> In his heart man plans his course, but the Lord determines his steps. (Proverbs 16:9 NIV)

Continuing on, we went to another location where there appeared to be a river of blood. The angel explained that it was the blood of believers who were killed because of their faith, and that their blood cries out to the Lord. This serves as a reminder that no one dies for their faith in vain, and that God sees everything, nothing is ignored.

Eventually, we found ourselves back at the river of life, and the angel disclosed that the river had the power to heal nations according to God's will.

We arrived at another location where I saw what appeared to be a large screen. The screen displayed events that were yet to happen in the world. As I watched, I saw a great and fierce war between nations.

The system of the world may let people believe that they are comfortable with their lives and that they are safe either because they have powerful armies or because they believe the world has never been as safe as it is in modern times.

But days are coming when wealth will not be the ultimate goal of life; people may want to enjoy life, but the system of the world will not allow that to happen. People will begin to discover that life is more than just accumulating wealth and trying to achieve all the material power that consumes the passions of almost everyone on earth. The wise will always be prepared, and they will put God and their faith in God first before they pursue any other goals.

"But seek first his kingdom and his righteousness, and all these things will be given to you as well" (Mathew 6:33 NIV).

Blessed are those who have discovered this truth and believe now, for the world will deteriorate more and more as the kingdom of God is about to be revealed. Most people have this signal in their consciousness, that the world will someday be on its knees, but most people choose to ignore it and live in denial. One day what is behind the unseen world will be revealed and a lot of people will be in regret, do not be one of them, set your priorities right.

"But the righteous will live by his faith" (Habakkuk 2:4).

In heaven, there is what looks like a massive structure where various spirits, chosen by God to reveal what is to come, convene at times. Here, future events are unveiled to the assembly. Although the servants of God in this world may not be aware that their spirits visit heaven occasionally, it is remarkable to see different servants of God from various parts of the world prophesying the same events that are to come. We have witnessed people uttering identical things before they materialize from different regions of the world, and they always come to pass.

After all these, Angel Raphael took me to the throne of the most high God. It was as big as I said before and the power around this place was so strong as if you could touch and feel the power with your hands.

There were great voices around and smoke with thunders inclusive. Surrounding the throne are angels that have spread their wings and are suspended high, and I was told that they do not move, and they have always been there since the creation of the world, and they love being in the presence of the great God.

While I was before the throne of God, I never saw the face of God, but I saw the feet and the hands which are very hard to describe in my own words as they were huge. What seemed to be the body was just fire all over. Some people end up describing God as fire when they see what I saw, but God is not fire.

It is actually, the glory beyond limits.

The glory is so much that even the eye of the spirit cannot see through and all it can see is fire. Every complex living being in heaven is always in awe of who God is and they all worship Him in His great majesty.

No person that ever existed before got to understand who really God is, what we know about God the creator of the universe is just small. The good thing is that He will reveal more of himself in the life to come when His kingdom is fully revealed.

I always think that God is unfathomable because He is so big and huge and having all powers and authority in this world. Yet He is mindful about us, and He is always watching over us day and night. He is the true definition of love.

I want to encourage everyone who feels like he/she is not good enough or strong enough to be close to God. The secret about following God is that He welcomes all who decide to follow Him. He doesn't choose who to accept or not. If you can only make a decision to follow Him, then His arms are wide open to accept and cherish you.

It doesn't matter if you are a believer or not, some people are believers, but they always see God from very far when He is in their hearts and all around them. God is more willing to accept you and you just have to come to Him the way you are and allow Him to love you to the end of the world. Just give God a place in your heart to love you and you will see how close you are to the almighty God of heaven and earth.

As I stood before the throne, I humbly worshipped God and prostrated myself face down. Suddenly, I felt a powerful force lifting me higher and higher until I was suspended in midair. As I looked to my right, I saw what appeared to be a screen within the vision, revealing a long table with numerous individuals feasting heartily. In the midst of them sat a man, who was addressing the gathering from a chair placed at the head of the table. At that moment, I heard a voice proclaiming, "A day will come when that feast will surely take place."

I was directed to turn my gaze to the opposite direction, and there before me was a vast expanse of fiery liquid, resembling either a lake or an ocean. Flames engulfed every inch of it, and it was seemingly bottomless. This was a warning of the fate that awaits those who reject God and His teachings. I witnessed individuals sinking into the inferno and resurfacing repeatedly, their agonizing screams piercing the air with relentless intensity.

I witnessed a figure resembling a son of man with eyes that glowed like fire. Although I could not clearly identify who he was, he spoke to me in a thunderous voice, delivering a message concerning these end times. The specifics of the message cannot be written in this book, as it is not meant to be revealed at this time.

As we strolled along the streets of heaven, we were surrounded by the magnificent beauty of God's kingdom. We encountered many people who had put their faith in God and had left this world behind, singing and dancing with unspeakable joy. I always encourage those who have lost loved ones in the Lord to take heart and rejoice, for their loved ones are in a wonderful place. If only they could see the splendor of heaven, they would long to be there too. As for me, I can hardly wait to be fully present with God, the angels, and all the saints. Although it may be beyond our understanding, it is the ultimate goal of life.

From this, Raphael led me to a room that was filled with an array of different wings. I observed that angels have the ability to move with or without wings, and our spirits can also be mobile with or without wings. Raphael then proceeded to replace the wings I had been using with a new pair, and it was an incredible experience that felt like Raphael was taking on big brother duties.

The Garden of Purpose

At last, we arrived at a massive garden filled with trees, and the angel accompanying me explained that each tree represented a different servant of God on Earth. Whenever an individual is chosen and commissioned to do God's work, a tree is planted in the garden. As the person carries out their mission, the tree grows and bears fruit. Once the fruit is ripe, it signifies the completion of the mission, and the person is then welcomed to their true home in heaven.

Those who follow God have been given a mission to accomplish on earth, which varies from person to person. For some, it might involve giving birth to someone who will later change the world while, for others, it could be helping a specific group of people. Some might have a mission in their businesses while others might have a purpose in their offices. And for some, their mission is to be messengers of God, sharing the Good News with people from different nations.

As you embark on your mission, a tree is planted to represent your purpose, and as you fulfill it, the tree grows and bears fruit. When the tree is fully grown and its fruits are ripe, you will be called back home to an amazing place. Many people are often perceived to not have lived their lives to the fullest, perhaps due to a premature death or unaccomplished goals.

From our earthly perspective, we may feel sad when someone passes away, especially if we believe they had more to accomplish in their life. However, in many cases, those who pass away in the hands of the Lord have actually fulfilled their mission and their tree is ripe.

Even though it may seem that they left things undone, they have truly lived their life to the fullest.

The ultimate goal of life is to be reunited with our Maker when all is said and done. During the vision, I was shown a staggering sight of a tree in a big garden that had the name of a great African prophet. For privacy reasons, I will not mention the name in this book. This detail has been in the book since it was first written in 2018. The vision was in 2014, and the tree had grown very well with fruits on half of its branches.

In that period, the great prophet from Africa was held in high regard by people all around the world, and his remarkable deeds in the name of God were widely celebrated. The news of his departure caught everyone by surprise, but he returned to his heavenly home. His passing came shortly after he had finished ministering the gospel in 2021. I, along with numerous others, had the privilege of witnessing his last moments as he preached on live television. It was a shocking turn of events, for just two hours after the service concluded, the heartbreaking news of his passing spread. Although the suddenness of it all was jolting, it became apparent that his tree had reached its fullness and ripeness.

The experiences I have shared above are meant to show you that God is more real than anything else in this world, and that His kingdom is more real than the kingdoms of this world. Hopefully, you can now see that God's perspective is often vastly different from the way we perceive things through our own limited understanding. As I bring this chapter to a close, I urge you to give yourself fully to God. He is aware of your current state as you read this book, and He knows your heart.

He is eager to establish a meaningful relationship with you.

"Now to him who is able to do immeasurably more than all we ask or imagine, according to his power that is at work within us, to him be glory in the church and in Christ Jesus throughout all generations, for ever and ever! Amen" (Ephesians 3:20–21 NIV).

CHAPTER 8

The Vision of Hell

Just about three years prior to the initial writing of this book, in 2015, I experienced another vision where I caught a glimpse of hell. Although it was not a detailed account, I had a significant conversation with the Lord during this vision. I am particularly fond of the message that was conveyed to me, and I have made the decision to include it in this book.

During my first year of college, I received an invitation to speak as a guest at a prayer joint meeting of SCOM, which involved some schools in the central region of Malawi. There were numerous students from different districts who had gathered to fellowship and pray together.

When it was my time to speak, I shared the testimony you are about to read. Upon finishing my speech, I witnessed students from different schools rushing to the front to surrender their lives to Jesus. The entire space in front was filled with these students, and it was amazing to witness these young people rediscover themselves for who they truly are. I hope that you will gain many insights as you read through this chapter.

One Saturday evening, while I was watching a TV documentary at home, I suddenly felt an overwhelming urge to sleep. Within seconds, I felt my spirit leave my body just like in previous visions. As I looked around, I saw someone standing beside me wearing a brilliantly shining white robe. In my spirit, I recognized Him as Jesus Christ, and He said to me, "Follow me, and I will show you."

As I followed Him, we entered a large, dark tunnel where even waving my hand in front of my eyes would not be seen. As we journeyed through the tunnel, we passed through gates, and Jesus spoke to me. As we continued, the temperature grew hotter, and I could hear terrible cries in the distance.

After passing through the gates, we continued down the dark tunnel until we reached what appeared to be an enormous auditorium. The size of it was difficult to comprehend, and it was filled with numerous pits, resembling the aftermath of severe soil erosion. As we entered the space, my eyes adjusted to the darkness, and I could see that the pits were filled with people crying out in agony of the fire in them. The sound of their cries was overwhelming and incessant. The suffering was so intense that I couldn't help but feel a deep sense of sadness and compassion for them.

I could also hear voices that were strong and strange and sounding very evil. The Lord revealed that the torments in hell are not limited to fire alone, but spirits also inflict pain upon those who find themselves there. The flames were wild and fierce, akin to that of gasoline, and could reignite as if someone poured gasoline over them. They burst like small bombs, scattered throughout the pits where anguished souls suffered.

As I was there, overwhelmed by the cries of the anguished souls, I heard my name being called out loud amidst the cries, "Kelliote, Kelliote!" The voices sounded familiar, but I couldn't place them. I couldn't help but feel sorrowful, thinking that these may be people who knew me when they were alive.

Feeling the weight of my sadness, I turned to the Lord and asked if there was any way to save these people from their torment. In response, the Lord pointed out that the only way to save people from hell is to prevent them from going there in the first place.

It is the responsibility of every believer to demonstrate love and compassion to others and assist them in avoiding hell by sharing the message of the kingdom. Sometimes, a simple act such as sharing a book with them, like this one, can aid in their self-discovery and assist them in avoiding eternal damnation.

Children of God, let's not get tired in sharing the good news with others, it is the best gift ever we can give to our loved ones and even strangers.

The Lord also emphasized to me that it is our responsibility to share the message while it is His responsibility to do the saving. We should not become overly involved and pushy in our approach. Rather, we just need to share the gospel message in a simple and straightforward manner. We do not require any complex or advanced message to reach out and talk to someone about Jesus. By sharing the message, we may be able to help someone escape the torment of hell.

The Lord also revealed to me that most people are unaware of the horrors that take place in hell because it's impossible for them to experience it firsthand. He explained that He allowed individuals like myself to have a glimpse of hell so that we could share the realities with others. I believe that's why I'm not the only one who has had this experience.

The Lord also revealed to me that there are many people in hospitals around the world who have been there for a long time, and even though some of them want to die, they haven't because the Lord is giving them more time to repent. This underscores the importance of sharing the good news even in hospitals.

I urge everyone to show kindness and concern to those in hospitals, even if they are not our family or friends. Additionally, I want to encourage those involved in hospital outreach ministries to persist in their efforts because there is a significant reward for doing so and others can be saved as a result. Although not everyone is called to do this type of work, if you feel the call to serve in this way, it may result in a tree being planted in your name to symbolize your mission and bring you joy.

The Lord emphasized that believing in Him is a personal choice and He doesn't impose it on anyone. He expressed the words, "Those who are ready to move with me, am ready to move them on," which meant that He is willing to lead and guide those who choose to follow Him.

Ultimately, it is up to the individual to declare their willingness to follow the Lord, and it is God's role to save and protect them. The

Lord also emphasized that God desires that no one should perish, but it is our decision to reject salvation and choose to perish.

As we were leaving, the Lord instructed me to share what I had witnessed with others. I felt uneasy because I knew that some people were skeptical about such testimonies, and I expressed my concerns to Him. I worried that people might believe that I was trying to scare them into believing by speaking about the terrors of hell.

He then said to me, "You don't have to frighten people about hell, warn them about hell."

As we made our way out, we encountered some formidable entities that appeared to be extremely aggressive. It was too dark in the tunnel to discern their features clearly, but they were frightful creatures, dragging people toward the direction we were coming out from. I could hear the cries of the people being dragged, screaming, "No! No! No!" It was heart-wrenching to witness their despair and realize that it was already too late for them.

Afterward, I suddenly woke up and felt as if I was reborn in my body. It seemed as though I had left my physical body and returned. Initially, I felt very weak, and my mind was unable to process things normally because it was all from the spiritual realm. Despite this, I managed to recall some of what had happened and decided to write it down and share it with others, as I had been instructed.

Today, I want to emphasize that hell is a real place, and the only way to avoid it is by accepting Jesus Christ as your savior. As a saved individual, it's important to share the good news of Jesus with others. Show them the love of God through your actions and words, and they will be drawn to that love. Sometimes, actions speak louder than words. When you demonstrate kindness and compassion toward others, it can be a powerful witness to the love of God.

I tell you that there is not any other way you can prevent eternal destruction apart from believing in God and His saving grace. As the Bible says in the following verse: "For God so loved the world that he gave his one and only Son, that whoever believes in him shall not perish but have eternal life" (John 3:16 NIV).

If you can only make the decision to receive Jesus today, then He is more than ready to move you on.

CHAPTER 9

The Rise of Persecution

I have included this chapter in my story to share some of the experiences that I went through during a sudden outbreak of persecution. With the grace that God had given me and my friends, there was a price to be paid.

In one of the previous chapters, I shared about how God had told me and my companions that every step that we took would be closely followed. We had been dedicated to doing God's work at our school, and we had witnessed many lives being transformed for the glory of God. However, things took a sudden turn, and every action we took seemed to trigger a negative reaction that resulted in further persecution.

The Precipitous Twist

Our school was a Catholic missionary secondary school that prioritized Catholic programs. We had a dedicated time during class hours for ethics meetings, where students of the same denomination gathered to pray. These meetings occurred once a week and were on the school timetable. SCOM, an interdenominational Christian organization, was open to all students, regardless of their religious affiliation. When I was in my senior year, I was chosen to lead SCOM.

During a Catholic ethics meeting, the Catholic patron (name withheld for privacy's sake) made an announcement that banned all Roman Catholic students from attending SCOM meetings. The patron alleged that SCOM members spoke with deceitful tongues and made false prophecies. They further accused SCOM members of putting demons into their own members instead of casting them out. Although I was uncertain about how or why they reached these conclusions, as the leader of SCOM, I felt the impact of these accusations most heavily.

Despite the patron's accusations, I firmly believed that our battle was not against human beings, but against evil forces, powers, and principalities. I was determined to continue to lead SCOM with integrity and continue our mission to serve God and our fellow students.

In a matter of days, my worst fear became a reality. Along with a group of students, I was summoned to the disciplinary room after our names were given to the headteacher and deputy headteacher. The headteacher is the equivalent of a school principal. The authorities accused us of causing confusion with our prayers. Apparently, someone reported us, and our names were surrendered to the school authorities. I suspected one occurrence that might have triggered this.

There was a time when it was a dark and eerie period in some of the hostels when a mysterious occurrence began. Whispers of a strange presence circulated among the students, and fear began to spread like wildfire. In the thick of the night, a liquid sucking sound would be heard, as if something was sucking blood on a person. Joseph confided in me that he had heard an unusual sucking sound at night in his hostel too, like someone was drinking through a straw. The worst part was that no one could identify the source of the sound, leaving everyone to wonder if it was a supernatural entity. For several days, the sound persisted, earning the name "blood sucker" from the terrified students. The tension in the hostel grew thicker, and everyone was on edge, dreading the onset of subsequent nightfall. The phenomenon always began with a nonstop vibration of the bed before the sucking sound pierced through the silence, making everyone who heard it freeze in fright.

In one still night, I was sleeping in my hostel, unaware of the horrors that had been plaguing other students in their hostels in the middle of the night. The darkness was blatant as there was a blackout when Joseph, with a look of fear etched on his face, suddenly came to me. He had come seeking help, for the "thing" had returned, and it was sucking blood again in his hostel. He implored me to give him the anointed materials that I had, which were said to be blessed by two great men of God from Africa. Think of these materials as the handkerchiefs of Paul in the Bible, believed to be point of contact with the power of God.

Just a few minutes after Joseph left, I lay awake in bed, still thinking about the strange occurrences in his hostel. Suddenly, I felt the bed on top of me start to vibrate like a phone call, but nonstop. My heart began to race. Then I heard the unmistakable sound of something sucking, coming from the bed above me where a form 1 student was sleeping. It was finally in my hostel.

I was paralyzed with fear, clutching my blankets tightly as I prayed silently. But as I prayed, the sound suddenly stopped and the thing jumped to another bed, repeating the vibrations and ensuing sucking noise. I could hear it moving around the room. It was as if an invisible presence was haunting us, preying on our fears. I continued to silently pray until it left.

The following night, I steeled myself and vowed not to be afraid if the "blood sucker" returned. However, it came again, and I heard the sucking sound coming from a bed adjacent to mine. This time, I immediately woke my roommates; and they, too, were terrified by the eerie sound. Determined to stop the mysterious occurrence, I called my friends, and we prayed outside the hostels, holding hands and speaking softly. In less than five minutes, everything was calm again.

This time, most of the students were awakened by the strange sound and after our prayer, they went back to their own beds. However, some were still afraid and refused to return to their hostels. They instead chose to sleep on the beds next to mine, believing that they would be safer if they slept closer to me. From this day, the thing never came back.

After the incident, some individuals reported us to the school authorities, and that is why we were called for disciplinary action as explained earlier. When we tried to explain what had happened, they couldn't comprehend it. They viewed us as religious fanatics and troublemakers.

The Climax

Every Monday, the school held assembly meetings where all students and teachers gathered in the school hall. During one such meeting, even after our disciplinary hearing, the headteacher addressed the issue of prayers. He patently expressed that some students were exaggerating their prayers, and that it was disturbing others who were trying to study. Furthermore, he warned that excessive prayer could also be detrimental to the students themselves, potentially causing them to fail in their academic pursuits.

It was unclear whether the headteacher's announcement was related to the previous incident or a new issue altogether, but it seemed as though they had heard false rumors that we were praying late at night and during study time. Though, I was always mindful of school schedules and never led prayers at inappropriate times. The headteacher went on to say that those who wanted to pray should wait until they were in theological college, adding, "This is not a theological college." The other students found this amusing; they all mockingly laughed, but I was not as hurt this time because I knew the battle had already been won.

Still, the humiliation was real.

The embarrassment I felt was immense since it was clear that the headteacher was referring to me and my friends. Such situations often caused me more emotional distress than the thought of encountering Satan in person.

As if the humiliation and fear caused by the assembly speech were not enough, things got even worse the next day. One by one, Andrew, myself, Joseph, Ernest, and Yohane were called to the head teacher's office. We were questioned about our alleged "exaggerated" prayers and accused of disrupting other students' studies. It was all unfounded, but the head teacher was determined to prove his point. To make matters worse, he called our parents to come to the school, making me anxious about what would happen next. The tension was intense, and I couldn't help but wonder what consequences we would face.

In a whirlwind of events, I was summoned to the deputy head teacher's office at approximately 5:30 p.m. on the same day. To my surprise, I found my mother waiting for me there. They proceeded to lecture me on the importance of prioritizing my studies over my prayers, urging me to reduce the time spent in prayer, yet prayer meeting time was just as it has always been at the school except that there was so much demonstration of God's power. I felt thoroughly disoriented and distressed by the sudden turn of events.

If a situation reached the point where your parents were called, it was clear that it was serious and that one's place in one of the best schools in the country could be at risk, a place that one can only attend with good grades. When my mother arrived, I could sense that most of what she was saying was an attempt to calm the deputy headteacher, who was known to be the strictest teacher at the school. She was negotiating to prevent them from suspending or expelling me from the school. She wanted me to accept most of the allegations, even though they were not true. Still, I knew the truth, so I refused to accept their false accusations and stuck to it. They eventually concluded that I should focus on my studies and reduce my prayers.

I found it remarkable how bold I was when speaking to those in authority, even in moments of fear. I felt the Holy Spirit fill me, and I stood firmly on what I knew to be true, boldly proclaiming my faith.

That week was particularly difficult for me as I struggled with confusion and emotional pain. At times, I would entertain thoughts like "What if they were right and I was just being stubborn?" Nevertheless, the words spoken by God and the encouragement from the angels He had sent to us helped to reassure me that the situation was not in my hands.

On the following Wednesday morning, I was still struggling with confusion and hurt, and to make matters worse, one of my friends was under attack by darkness. It was a serious test, but Joseph and I felt compelled to pray for him outside of school hours. I was extremely fearful as I had just been warned about praying, and here

I was, only a day later, breaking the rule. My heart and mind were in turmoil, and I could only rely on God's strength to carry me through.

During that week, specifically on a Thursday, I could feel a heightened sense of spiritual warfare in my spirit. Something was definitely not right, and I knew we were under attack. In the afternoon, Yohane's mother arrived at the school to discuss the same issue. His mother shouted at him, and the troubled look on his face afterward was evident. As a result of the confrontation, Yohane was forbidden from attending SCOM and any non-Catholic church. This prohibition had an immediate impact on our plans for the upcoming weekend, as we were supposed to attend a prayer event at another school. Sadly, Yohane was prevented from joining us.

The prayer function scheduled for the weekend was a regular gathering of students for joint prayer and fellowship. Yohane's family were strict Catholics, and that's why he was prohibited from attending any more non-Catholic prayers. During the disciplinary session, he told me how his mother shouted at him before the authorities and even slapped him.

At a certain point, Yohane was summoned by his family to be disciplined in front of a group of relatives. He confided in me that he was feeling down because they insulted him and gave him many derogatory names. They even claimed that his involvement in prayers was the cause of his poor academic performance, which was not the case. Overwhelmed by everything, he had to step away from his participation in the activities that we used to do together as friends at school.

To add to the challenges we were already facing, the following week brought yet another ordeal. One Tuesday night, a school authority responsible for student well-being made rounds in all the classes.

During the mandatory silent study time, when everyone was supposed to be quietly focused on their studies, this authority singled us out indirectly in his repeated speech and criticized us for the very same thing they had never actually witnessed. It felt like an unnecessary and unfair targeting of us.

He established his own regulations for the school, which included a ban on group activities during non-academic hours and requiring groups to register with him. Additionally, he forbade the spreading of negative prophecies among students. Although he may have received reports of incidents that he had not witnessed personally, his rules seemed to be targeted at me and my friends. It was a discouraging time for me, as I had never been so embarrassed by a misunderstanding that had caused so much uproar. From the headteacher to the deputy and other officials, everyone appeared to be furious with us.

Our reputation in school had changed, and not for the better. We had become famous for the wrong reasons, and people started giving us mocking nicknames. Even some teachers joined in the mockery, and it seemed like everyone was laughing at us.

I recall an incident when I overheard some fellow students gossiping about me in the dining hall. They had no idea that I was sitting at the next table, listening to everything they said. When they eventually noticed me, I simply smiled and didn't say a word. It was clear to me that such battles are not meant to be fought in the physical, and I didn't want to stoop to their level by engaging in gossip or confrontation.

On another occasion, I was lying on my bed in my room, and a few students were in the hostel having a heated argument about me. They were unaware that I was inside the room. Some believed that my actions were from God while others argued that it was all fake. The debate went on for a long time, and I quietly listened without saying a word. Eventually, many of my fellow students came to the realization that we had been sent by God to the school to spread the Gospel.

In June and July of 2014, I sat for my final secondary school exams, and it was an exhilarating experience to see how well I performed. The moment of truth came when I went to check my results, and to my surprise, it was the headteacher himself who informed me of my performance. As I entered his office, he greeted me with a smile and couldn't wait to share the news. With a gleam in his eyes, he exclaimed, "I have seen your name, you are one of the top performers!" Overwhelmed with joy, I couldn't find the right words to express my feelings, so I simply returned the smile, trying my best to be humble.

I always thank God for Mrs. Manda, who stood by us when there was a lot of negativity surrounding the work we did. As the patron of SCOM, she used to tell us how some other members of staff would talk about us even in their offices. Despite this, she encouraged my friends and me to pray even more, saying that God would give us victory one day. I remember visiting her after the exam results were out, and she shared with me how some members of staff were asking her what she was doing to help her SCOM students pass exams. I couldn't help but find it ironic.

It is remarkable that all my close friends have been promoted by God. At the time, I wrote this book for the first time, Joseph was in South Africa, pursuing further education and working with his parents in ministry, as his father was a pastor. Similarly, Yohane had graduated from a school in India and was pursuing his master's degree at another institution in the same country.

Ernest was studying for his degree at the Malawi University of Science and Technology, one of the top universities in Malawi, while Emmanuel was pursuing his degree at Chancellor College, which is also among the top universities in the country.

Andrew moved to India after finishing his studies in Malaysia to pursue further education in Shimla. Meanwhile, I was in my third year of pursuing a degree in agricultural and applied economics at Lilongwe University of Agriculture and Natural Resources. By God's grace, at the age of twenty-five, I completed my first master's degree in business administration online from India and was based in New Jersey, USA, pursuing another master's degree in organization development at Cairn University in Pennsylvania. There were some individuals in my social circles who were curious about how I managed to pursue two master's degrees simultaneously without feeling overwhelmed. I believe that if they read this book, they would understand my secret.

It is fascinating how the very same people who were mocked for their faith in God were later elevated by Him for His own glory.

This can only be attributed to the work of God; no one ever loses by standing up for God, no matter where they are.

Standing up for God is a decision that should never be feared, as He is always present to back you up, even if you can't see it at the time when it's most needed. It's important to understand that His support is always there. With Jesus by your side, there's no need to be anxious about the future.

CHAPTER 10

Q & A

In the feedback, I have received about my experiences, I have noticed that many people ask similar questions. Therefore, in the final section of this book, I have compiled some of these frequently asked questions and provided my best answers based on my knowledge and experience.

Question 1

Do you still have the visions and the experiences happening to you now?

Answer

To address this inquiry, I will share an important message that an angel conveyed to me and my companions after our experience. The angel explained that God had sent them to have an intimate interaction with us for a specific period of time, to instruct and equip us for the future. The angel also mentioned that since the mission was fulfilled, we would not have that same close encounter again. However, we were to remember that God always has His angels surrounding every believer, and they are constantly with us.

After that time, we noticed a decrease in the frequency of unusual occurrences and experiences. It was rare to see something strange happening in the sky or have a close interaction with an angel. However, what stayed with me was a renewed and personal relationship with God. I still have the ability to see visions that are mostly related to my personal life and many times hear the voice of the Holy Spirit, which has been a constant in my life ever since.

The majority of the crucial decisions that I make are based on insights from the unseen realm. This has been the most beneficial aspect of my experiences since it has made my life easier, as I follow God's voice, which is clear to me based on what I have experienced. I am not implying that life has been smooth sailing for me, but I am confident because I know that God is always by my side.

During my second year in college, there was a time when I was very depressed due to something that happened during that period. One night, I found myself sitting alone in the dark outside one of the buildings on campus, feeling very cold and lost. I turned to God in my heart and asked Him to help me. Suddenly, I was hit by a powerful energy in my spirit and felt an electric sensation run through my body. My spiritual eyes opened, and I saw an angel standing in front of me, who told me not to worry and then took out a fruit from his hand and gave it to me to eat. As I consumed the fruit, I felt the depression melting away instantly, like ice under the sun. It was truly a miraculous experience that left me feeling uplifted and grateful for God's intervention.

Instantly, I was overwhelmed with joy and peace as I felt the presence of God with me. I heard His voice asking me, "What do you want me to do for you?" Without hesitation, I told Him my request, and He replied that it was already done.

As soon as I got up from where I was, I returned to my room feeling overjoyed. Amazing things started happening to me that week as I saw God fulfilling what I had asked for. This is just one of the many incredible ways God has continued to reveal Himself in my life since the events described in this book.

On occasion, I receive straightforward directions like "Send a text message to this person and check on their well-being" or "Donate all of your saved money to help others." These instructions are conveyed to me distinctly, and each time I follow through, incredible things happen, even though the outcome may take some time to come to pass. I hear the voice of God as the following verse affirms: "My sheep hear my voice, and I know them, and they follow me" (John 10:27 ESV).

To conclude and respond to the question, I can say that I continue to have personal experiences with God, similar to many other believers who experience His communication. I firmly believe that the ability to communicate with God is one of the most powerful gifts He has given to believers.

Question 2

How sure are you that what you have experienced is true and worth believing?

Answer

In my personal opinion, the confirmation of the Holy Spirit within my heart, affirming the truthfulness of these lessons, provides me with the assurance and confidence to believe that they are indeed true and worth believing in. The sense of peace and joy that accompanies each experience further solidifies my conviction that I have encountered the presence of God, as stated in the following Bible verse: "Now the Lord is the Spirit, and where the Spirit of the Lord is, there is freedom" (2 Corinthians 3:17 ESV).

Experiencing visions, interacting with angels, or feeling the presence of God is a truly remarkable phenomenon that cannot be described in words. It refreshes my spirit, fills my heart with immense joy, and brings an unexplainable sense of peace. I believe that this sense of freedom is the result of being in the presence of the Holy Spirit, and it is what gives me complete confidence.

In addition to this, there are other factors that further strengthen my belief in what I have witnessed. These include physical signs that God has provided, which prove beyond any doubt that what He revealed is worthy of belief. I have already discussed some of these signs in previous chapters. In addition to that, while in high school,

I once saw a vision that involved my future and initially had doubts about its meaning. An angel in the vision assured me that God would provide a sign to confirm its validity.

The following day, while walking with Joseph, Angel Michael instructed me to look up. To my amazement, I saw a large, clear letter *S* formed in the clouds, which represented my middle name, Samuel. The angel then spoke, saying, "You wanted a sign. That's it!"

Yohane also had a vision when he was alone, and he was in disbelief of what he saw. As a result, he couldn't speak anymore, and no sound could come out of his mouth. He was instructed to find me and request that I pray for him. Later on, he found me, but he still couldn't speak, so he wrote a note on a piece of paper, explaining his situation. He wrote that he couldn't speak because he didn't believe, and he needed me to pray for him. I prayed for him to regain his voice, and he began to speak again and regained his belief. Witnessing his restoration boosted my faith as well.

Another way that increases my confidence in what I experienced is how some of the things that were revealed to me have come to pass over the years. For instance, I had a vision where I saw myself flying in a plane, specifically in America, and I wrote it down in my diary in 2014. At that time, it seemed impossible to me that such a thing could ever happen. However, seven years later, I found myself flying over the buildings of New York City and landing at JFK International Airport for the first time, just as I had seen in the vision.

Yohane was told that one day he would go to India. In 2014, that never made sense, but two years later, he got a scholarship from the Indian government to go and study in India. These and many other occurrences, that not even chance would be a suitable word to explain them, also give me confidence to believe in what I have heard and seen to be true.

Question 3

Is your family aware of these experiences? Do they get involved?

Answer

My family is fully aware of everything. Whenever I returned home from school, I used to share with my parents about all that was happening at school. Also, we used to have family prayers at night before going to bed, and during prayers, I would share the things I saw in my visions that were coming ahead, and we would pray together.

At times, I prayed for my sick family members, and they were instantly healed. I faced challenges when trying to explain to my family that I followed what I believed the Spirit was leading me to do, not what others expected of me. Sometimes my family or friends wanted me to pray or minister to others because of my experiences, but I only did what I felt led to do. By the time I turned sixteen, I was already ministering in our local church, and during these times, the presence of God touched both the young and old. My family was fully aware of these experiences.

I recall receiving a message from my younger brother while I was in college. He shared with me how he shared my testimony with one of his classmates, which led the classmate to believe in Jesus. Additionally, one of my uncles received an early copy of my testimony during a visit to our home. He then shared it with the pastor's wife at his church, who was so moved by it that she invited me to speak at their church.

During my third and fourth year in college, my parents shared some of the first copies of my testimony with their friends and other interested people. When I returned home, I was surprised to find people I didn't know personally requesting to meet me. My family has always been involved in my journey and provided unwavering support in many ways. So to answer the question, yes, my family is fully supportive and involved in my experiences and endeavors.

Question 4

What can anyone do to have an experience with God? Did you do anything in particular to experience these things?

Answer

I believe that my life is not exceptional or unusual. I had a typical upbringing, much like other children in the southern part of Malawi. In my childhood, I was quite mischievous and got into trouble often, leading my parents to discipline me severely. I was known as the "ninja" in my neighborhood because of my reputation for fighting and winning most of the fights I engaged in, especially when I was between the ages six and ten.

What I am trying to convey is that my upbringing was nothing extraordinary, just that of an average Malawian kid from the ghetto. As I mentioned in previous chapters, it was during my high school years that I started to explore my faith more deeply. During that time, I was simply inquisitive and wanted to learn more about God through scripture. I was like any other typical believer, spending time in prayer, reading and reflecting on the scriptures, and engaging in other common Christian practices.

There is nothing really special that I can remember or think of that I did to experience any of these things, I just see the grace of God. I believe God can choose anyone to experience the same.

If someone desires to experience God, I advise them to prioritize the scripture above all else. The scripture holds immense power in a believer's life. Trusting in what God has stated in His word can transform a person's life and provide them with an incredible encounter with God. The way in which God's Word can bring individuals closer to God is truly remarkable.

Numerous theological and logical debates surround the scripture, but personally, I embrace the simplicity of it. I trust the Word of God as it is and through this comes peace and enlightening revelations. I strongly hold that the Word of God is one of the most powerful gifts bestowed upon mankind and it is efficacious, bearing fruits.

"Heaven and earth will pass away, but my words will not pass away" (Matthew 24:35 ESV).

As an individual who has had some experience with God behind the unseen world, my top preference has always been the Word of God.

This is because I can always access God's Word through scripture whenever I desire, and there appears to be a connection between comprehending God's Word through scripture and encountering God beyond the natural realm.

In conclusion, knowing and believing in God's Word as revealed in the scriptures is crucial to experiencing God. It is only through the understanding and application of God's teachings that one can truly have a personal relationship with Him.

CLOSING WORDS

This book has been written with the intention of revealing to you the extent of God's investment in your life and the immeasurable value that all Christians hold in God's eyes. My hope is that, through the words written here, your faith will be lifted above any fear or doubt and that you will be empowered to stand strong against the lies and schemes of the devil and his forces.

However, I must remind you that while the insights shared in this book can aid your understanding of God's Word, it should never replace the Holy Bible as the ultimate source of truth. It is essential that you continue to hold fast to the Word of God and allow this book to supplement your understanding rather than replace it.

As you embark on this journey of deeper understanding and connection with God, I wish you all the best and pray that the wisdom shared in these pages will bring you closer to His heart.

SALVATION PRAYER

If you have read this book and feel that you are not in a right relationship with God and that you need Jesus in your life, I encourage you to say this prayer:

"Dear Lord Jesus, I believe that you died for my sins and rose again for my salvation. Today, I surrender my life to you and make you the Lord and Savior of my life. I believe that I am now born again and will forever be in your care. In Jesus's name, amen!"

ABOUT THE AUTHOR

Kelliote is a firstborn in a Christian family of four. He was born and raised in Malawi, a country in the southeastern part of Africa. When this book was published, he was in New Jersey, United States, of America. Throughout his life from his teenage years, he has always had a passion for helping people discover themselves through understanding the ways of God. This passion has led him to minister the Word of God and transform many lives in Malawi and beyond. Throughout this process, God has manifested his ways and teachings to Kelliote in peculiar ways. Through these understandings, many people have received spiritual freedom and enlightenment as they discover the ways of God in special ways. Many others have come to know God and accepted Jesus as they get impacted by the realities of the spiritual world and the Word of God. Kelliote continues to share the realities about God's kingdom and His love upon His people on earth as God has gifted him.

Printed in the USA
CPSIA information can be obtained
at www.ICGtesting.com
CBHW021159190724
11674CB00002B/282